Mystic Mel
behind the eight ball

"*Life is ten percent what happens to you
And ninety percent how you react to it*"
Charles R. Swindall

Behind the Eight Ball: The Marvelous Misadventures of Mystic Mel by Ronald Melvin

Copyright © 2018 by Ronald Melvin

Cover by: Stephen Woodin Sr.

234p. 18ill. cm.

ISBN 978-1-935795-54-4

LCCN 2018948987

All Rights Reserved. This book is a work of fiction. No part of this book may be reproduced, stored in a retrieval system, or transmitted in any form or by any means, electronic, mechanical, photocopying, recording, or otherwise, without permission in writing from Michael Ray King Publishing

Michael Ray King Publishing
PO Box 353431
Palm Coast, FL 32135-3431

Printed in the United States of America

This book is dedicated to my family, including those who have passed: my parents, Albert and Evelyn Melvin and my sister Evelyn. To those who are still here providing me with love and support: my sister Cheryl, my daughters Ronte` and Samantha, my son-in-law Mickey and my granddaughter, Brennan

Table of Contents

Acknowledgements

Forewords

Dave Hollingshead
DTM (Distinguished Toastmaster)
PID (Past International Director, Toastmasters)

Dennis E. Wooldridge
DTM
Past International Director & District 84 Governor

Introduction

Sweet Home Alabama 1
Family Secrets 7
Life Lessons Begin 16
Grandma's Church 20
The Wisdom of Grandma 31
Nobody Knows What Trouble I See 35
Famous Last Words: 'Watch This' 43
Lessons of the Father 46
Dad's Brothers, Tom and Leroy 50
Talking about the Ghetto 51
Josh 59
Lesson Learned 61
The Village 64
Great Expectations 66
Dad, the Coach and Mel 68
Channeling Mom and Dad 71
Bruce 76

Want Respect, Give Respect 86
Sean's Wife's Birthday Present 88
Hey, My Man 93
Welcome to my World 97
Bikers for First Amendment Rights 99
      (BFFAR – Crazy Charlie)
Willie 105
Becoming a Blue Blood 108
What KKK Rally? 111
I Didn't Raise You That Way 115
My New Support Family 122
The Adventures of Steve and Mel 128
A Friendship Grows 131
The Creation of Wedding Phobia 134
Snowmobile X Games 140
"Want to see a pencil float?" 146
The Legend of the Inflatable Doll 154
Steve's Phantom Breakfast 160
A Moment of Karma 162
Captain Mel 165
RENT-A-COP 176

      Collection of Miscellaneous Stories 179

We May Never Meet Again 180
The Power of Small Deeds 185
Article from local Toastmasters newsletter 187
Palm Coast Observer 193
How to Win the Toastmasters World Championship of Public Speaking 200
About the Author 213

Acknowledgements

This product of love could not have been completed without the help and support of many people. I'd like to take this opportunity to thank some special friends. They pushed from the back while having one hand around my neck. It takes that extra effort to motivate me.

Here's a special shout out and thank you to two ladies who served as my proof readers: thank you Gloria DeBusman and Pat Linehan.

Thanks to Don Sumner for holding my feet to the fire. Don knew how to keep me focused.

Steve Woodin and Bob, your design of the book cover was marvelous even though you threatened to make me disappear if I didn't use it.

Thank you to all my Toastmaster family. With their support I never gave up. Especially Dave Hollingshead and Dennis Wooldridge.

A very, very special thank you to Sherry Greene who did the majority of the typing and the initial and on-going proofing and reading of the manuscript.

Last but certainly not least, thank you to Michael Ray King the catalyst, the motivator and publisher of *Behind the Eight Ball*. Mike says there is a book in every person. He was my inspiration.

The names and the places in the stories have been changed to protect me so I don't get sued. (Wink, wink!) That's the truth!

Foreword #1

I've had the privilege to know Ron "Mystic Mel" Melvin for a number of years through our membership in the Toastmasters organization. In addition to being a gracious and kind man, Ron is gifted with superior speaking talent, as well as also being a natural entertainer. Ron merges both these skills effortlessly in his work as a magician.

I recall one especially humorous magic trick involving a banana and a bandana! Ron's facial expressions and vocal variety was priceless as he performed the illusion! I still do not know how he did it … and he will not tell.

As talented as Ron is as a magician, he is even more talented as a speaker. I was in the audience in 2012, and watched and cheered as Ron participated as one of the nine finalists in the Toastmasters International World Championship of Public Speaking. At that final level of the competition, there is very little "daylight" between any of the contestants, and I saw little that day between any of the nine on stage. Only an elite few, the "best of the best" earn the right to compete at this level! Ron proved himself an elite speaker and delivered an outstanding presentation on that day.

In Ron's book *Behind the Eight Ball*, Ron addresses some of his more memorable misadventures which provided fodder for many of Ron's speeches. You will find yourself laughing heartily as Ron recounts stories such as not being aware of what to expect when he found himself the only person of color in attendance at a Lynyrd Skynyrd concert, or how he handled the situation while flying in a small plane when the pilot managed to knock himself out, along with a series of other misfortunate events.

Prepare to be entertained and enjoy the adventure as you dive into Ron's latest novel, *Behind the Eight Ball*.

Dave Hollingshead
DTM (Distinguished Toastmaster)
PID (Past International Director, Toastmasters)

Foreword #2

I met Ronald "Mel" Melvin several years ago while we were in Toastmasters...no need to focus on how many years. I have come to know him as an open, kind and genuine human being, a talented speaker and skillful magician. I was delighted when Ron asked me to write an introduction to his book. When I was the District Governor of Toastmasters District 84, Ron worked his way up through the various contest from club to District.

He won the District contest with a wonderful speech and was on his way to the semi-finals of Toastmaster's World Championship of Public Speaking. This is a goal of tons of Toastmasters including myself. Ron accomplished something unparalleled in the history of the District...he won his semi-final and became one of the nine finalists from across the globe, and more importantly from a local perspective the first finalist from District 84.

He did all the work and we were busting our buttons. And as icing on the cake, the Convention where the finals would be held was in our own back yard, Orlando. I remember having dinner with Ron the night after the semi-finals. Knowing he would be on the "big stage" on Saturday, well he was a bit like a long-tailed cat in a room full of rocking chairs. He did himself and the District proud from that stage that morning, and I will always be proud of the way he performed and represented the District.

In *Behind the Eight Ball* Ron opens the doors and the windows to his life so you the reader will get to know him better. Family, friends and others from his life populate the pages. His simple way of storytelling and the life lessons he gifts to us the readers reflect the man I have come to know and appreciate. I am sure you will enjoy the book as much as I did.

Dennis E. Wooldridge
DTM (Distinguished Toastmaster)
Past International Director & District 84 Governor

Introduction

I was born and raised in Philadelphia. Our family was the first black family to locate into an all Irish community and growing up I believed I was Irish. It was great. I became just another kid on the block. My family members were startled when I developed an Irish brogue. Having two godmothers, one Irish and one black, you could say I was spoiled. My Irish godmother immersed me in the Catholic traditions, to the chagrin of my Baptist mother.

In time, the community metamorphosed from an Irish neighborhood into an all-black community.

Although black myself, when the community changed I became the odd-ball and found it difficult at times to fit in. This would follow me the rest of my life. I had to learn that not everyone accepted me. There were neighborhoods I was not to visit. God knows I wasn't allowed on American Bandstand, even though it was just a couple of miles away.

IBM hired me in 1966, which was during the civil rights era. That was when I was introduced to the real world of racism. Some companies would not let me onto their property. Others called the company telling them not to send me back. I would always call before arriving and you could see the shock on their faces when I showed up. I didn't 'sound' black.

Even with those challenges, I earned IBM's highest service award twice. I worked hard and earned the respect of my peers.

My move to Minnesota was a shock to both native Minnesotans and to myself. The first years were very trying. Those years were full of lessons and personal growth. During that time the community and I learned to respect each other. Over time, I became the chair of the Human Rights Commission for the city of Rochester and later for the whole county.

As one of the first, and few, persons of color in Rochester, Minnesota, IBM asked me to present and share my experiences. When I retired from IBM I was asked to be the resource director for the United Way. Again, I had to give presentations. I joined Toastmasters to hone my speaking skills. To hold the audience's attention, I learned magic. Brent Coggins, a professional magician, took me under his wing. The rest is history.

When I joined Toastmasters, I used my misadventures for my presentations. I could find a story to fit any situation. To my delight my fellow Toastmasters found them inspiring, enlightening and highly entertaining. The more I spoke, the more my repertoire of stories grew. Toastmasters provided me with a means to remember and share my personal stories.

During my years in Toastmasters I discovered the world of competitive speaking. Then came a personal tragedy which I shared with my Toastmaster family. It was a form of therapy, turning that tragedy into an inspirational presentation, which became the winning vehicle that propelled me to the International Championship of Public Speaking.

In 2012 I was recognized as of the nine top speakers in the world. The contest had begun with 33,000 contestants. With my competitive success came speaking opportunities. This was the moment I realized that the stories of my life could inspire others. Michael Ray King, a Toastmaster and publisher, suggested that I compile my stories in a book.

Come along as I reveal how I survived unscathed after my curious experiences. Was it a divine presence or my childlike mentality? Share in my exposure to different cultures, ethnic groups, hobbies and challenging experiences.

Why the title *"Behind the Eight Ball?"* My daughter, Ronte`, explains it best.

"This *(the title)* speaks to playing pool: sinking all numbered balls except the eight ball. However, if one of your shots found you with a numbered ball behind the eight ball, this would be a skilled shot, requiring you to look at all ways to sink the numbered ball without sinking the eight ball with it. Your stories convey this idea; finding yourself in humorous, scary, baffling situations in which you are behind the eight ball. How do I get out alive, how do I get out and not injure myself or highlight stereotypes or prejudices?

The manner in which these stories are told allow the reader to easily see the situation and cheer on your success in getting out. A reader can bring to mind their own 'eight ball' moment and recall how they got out. Be that with humor, quick wit or prayer, I'm sure we can all recall an eight-ball moment and how we successfully prevailed." *(I'd take credit for this except she's going to read the book.)*

After reading my exploits, I believe you will agree.

Thank you, may you enjoy my stories.

Live long and prosper.

Sweet Home Alabama
(Jack Daniels and Hand Rolled Cigarettes)

Minnesota winters can be brutal! The cold, the wind, snow and thirty-plus days without any sun. All part of nine and a half months of winter. According to the Minnesota Department of Natural Resources, the record low temperature for Minnesota was minus sixty degrees on  February 2, 1996. That didn't include the wind chill. By the way: the maximum high temperature is 115F. How can one place get that cold and that hot? Did I mention the cold?

When it gets down to -35F you see the world differently. I've seen a video of boiling water thrown outside at that temperature. The water morphed into a puff of smoke, never to be seen again.

I recall a time when I was sitting in my car. The window fogged up instantly, then I noticed my breath. There was nothing unusual about seeing my breath because of the subfreezing temperatures. What was different this time is that it was so cold that I was shocked seeing my breath change to snowflakes and fall to my lap.

You may be thinking that can't be true. Black folks don't live in Minnesota. Actually, you are correct. I now live in Palm Coast, Florida. Okay, that was my attempt at ethnic humor. Although that was a joke it felt that way during my time I lived in Rochester, Minnesota. Rochester had 110,000 people of which 400 were of color. This count included men, women and children.

My white friends thought all black people in town knew each other. That's because when two black people crossed paths in public they greet each other like they were long lost friends. Of course, we didn't know each other. We were just so happy to see someone who looked like us!

As a result, I developed different tastes. For instance, my love of lutefisk and Polka music. Okay, another attempt at ethnic humor. I did develop a liking for Texas blues. One of the bands high on my list was ZZ Top. I loved their driving, bluesy rock and roll sound.

I was always looking for something to do during the long winter months. I was elated when I heard ZZ Top was scheduled to perform in Minneapolis, which is about 90 minutes from Rochester. That would be a little over an hour and a half drive. I began the task of shifting things in my busy schedule to make time for some personal entertainment. I bought a ticket.

Arriving at the venue, I observed that it was in the basketball arena. I took my seat on the left side of the stage about ten rows up from the floor. The seat was approximately midway from the front of the stage. This gave me full view of everything except what was directly behind me. It didn't take long before I realized I was the only person of color in attendance.

There wasn't a person of color anywhere including the support staff. The arena filled quickly. Just before the show started, the announcer shared that there were 33,000 people in the house. I thought to myself, 33,000 and me. That's when the lights went down.

 ZZ Top took to the stage. They played a driving, jamming set filled with all my favorite songs. I was filled with excitement when they customarily rotated their guitars. When they completed their set and left the stage for intermission, I thought that this would be a good time to leave. After giving it some thought I decided, why drive back so quickly? Even though I was busy at work, why not take a little more time for myself? Right? I mean, what could happen?

The next group to perform was not well known to me. The band's name was Lynyrd Skynyrd. I was familiar with some of their music. Hey, I paid my money, so why not stay for the full show? The lights dimmed again and out on the stage came a gnarly looking band. I don't remember what their opening song was, but it wasn't bad. When the applause quieted down, the leader of the band who was holding a bottle of Jack Daniels, took center stage. He grabbed the mic and shouted, "There won't be any God damn rap music in the house tonight."

The crowd yelled and screamed with agreement. My stress increased. He then announced that they were going to "take it down home." Then from behind the band the largest Confederate battle flag I have ever seen unfurled from the ceiling. It covered the full stage from the top to the bottom and from left stage to right stage. I knew this was it. I'm going to die!

The audience went wild. The band began to play Sweet Home Alabama. The crowd exploded. Jumping to their feet, they were all singing along with the band. At that point, I was hoping they were not going to have a Civil War flashback. Inside I could feel myself freaking out. Through the noise of the crowd I heard my father's voice, saying "when in Rome do as the Romans do." I jumped up and joined in singing "Sweet Home Alabama." The next thing I knew, the people on either side of me had their arms around my shoulders as we swayed back and forth to the rhythm of the melody. We were really getting into that song! That's when they introduced me to one of their friends - Jack Daniels. Jack and I are good friends to this day.

The band played through their repertoire. My new friends became even friendlier. I observed that these were hard working blue-collar folks who don't have a lot of money. What brought me to this conclusion? I noticed they were not only rolling their own cigarettes, they were sharing them! Then they passed them down the row. It was shared with me even though I didn't smoke. Yep, I inhaled. As the night progressed our time together became the center of the universe. We shared a wonderful experience that evening, singing, laughing and having the best time of our lives.

As the concert concluded, the men shook my hand and the women gave me hugs. Of course, we promised to meet again some time. We then went our separate ways.

I don't remember how long or far I traveled down the highway. When I began to reminisce about that great evening, special moments of the event began to bounce around inside my head. That's when I had a second visit from my father. I felt like my father had slapped me in the back of the head. It was one of those "Ah ha" moments. I had had a remarkable learning experience.

You see, it dawned on me when entering that arena I was the one who was the racist, bigot and judge. Those people had come to enjoy themselves. I wasn't even on their radar. They accepted me as one of them because I was there for the music. There was no judgment of me. The music became our common ground. No matter what other misunderstandings - politics, religion or ethnicity - that was what was important. We were there for the music.

When you're stepping into a new situation or meet someone for the first time, seek common ground. I'm not speaking of compromise. Because compromise is when one or both have to give up something. That can happen later. I'm speaking of something you both already like or agree upon. Spend some time with common ground before moving on to the differences or the unknowns.

I'm betting that you will have a better experience, make more new friends, find negotiations easier, obtain new clients and have less discord in your relationships. All this by seeking common ground first.

Now, when I'm in a difficult situation, I find myself humming "Sweet Home Alabama" silently to myself. "Sweet home Alabama."

If you wish to tell a secret in your home, make sure that even your servant's shoe is out. **Greek**

Family Secrets

Each family has its secrets. When I was a young man, families would not wash their linen in public. This meant that most family concerns were kept within the family. Today it seems that the more dirty laundry a person owns, the more hits they get on Twitter.

Mom and Dad

My family was no different than any other. In fact, many of the secrets were only shared to me after a relative passed away. My grandmother was full of secrets. Most of them she took to the grave.

Part of her life I know was spent in New York City. Whether she owned the building she lived in or not I don't know. But I know that she managed a brownstone in New York City. She was married at that time to my grandfather, Jasper. Jasper, from the stories I've been told, was definitely a very shady person. He was always trying to make quick money. Quick money is rarely made legally.

By my grandmother's account, one day he returned home and said they had to move. This meant that she had to take a little baby, my mother, and leave town immediately. This also meant that she left most of her belongings. They moved to Philadelphia.

Grandmother became a live-in maid. Granddad was still getting into trouble. He spent long periods of time in the penal institution. Grandmother's child, my mother, had to be farmed out. My mother stayed with several families while Grandmother spent time performing her duties.

Grandmother must've been very good at what she did. When I was old enough to understand, I realized that she owned her own home. This means that this was a black woman in a white neighborhood owning her own home. There is a story there I'm sure, but no one has shared it with me. I may never know the story because very few of my family are still alive.

While Grandmother worked hard to provide a living it meant she was rarely home to take care of her child. So my mother lived with other families, my grandmother paying them for her room and board. I believe this nomad life led to her mental instability. When I was old enough, my mother shared with me that these families did not treat her well. They used the money for themselves. She was treated very badly.

Growing up I realized my mother had several medical problems. One was migraine headaches and I knew that she would go away for a while. That's when Dad would have to take care of the family. This was a horrible time for us kids. Dad could not cook. When he did 'cook' he put everything in the same pan, at the same time. He did not like washing dishes. And we lived under martial law. Recently, I have found out that my mother suffered from depression. She could have possibly been bipolar. Her time away from home was spent recovering her mental health.

Grandmother, at some point, realized that leaving my mother with another family was not in the best interest of her daughter. My mother was sent to a boarding school in Bordentown, New Jersey. The school went by the same name and was built on the same foundation, values and beliefs of Tuskegee Institute.

Men and women wore uniforms while at the school and were trained in a trade or vocation, which was second only to learning social skills. Each student left the school qualified to enter their chosen profession.

My mother became a seamstress. She was expert at what she did. I remember her taking a Vogue pattern and changing its size. It was a woman's size and my mother cut it down to fit my sister for her prom.

To this day it is still a family secret of whom is my biological father. What I do know from bits and pieces of conversations is that my mother became pregnant by a man who was married. This was not found out by my grandmother until the day of my mother's wedding. The complete story remains unknown to me.

When my grandmother was in an assisted living facility I would visit her whenever I had the opportunity. One day when we were alone sitting together, I asked Grandmother, "What was my father like?"

She said, "Oh, he was a good man."

I responded with, "What did he do, was he a carpenter or into construction?"

She looked off into the distance. Replying to me she said he did the best he could. That was the end of that conversation.

The man I call my father must have met my mother after I was born. This was right after the Second World War. An unmarried woman with a child at this time was taboo. But my father fell totally in love with my mother. I do believe he also fell in love with me.

There are some things about my culture that are not readily shared. Even though we speak of prejudice coming from the white community, we have a strong prejudice streak within our own community. One of them is about the shades of our skin. The other is about the texture of our hair. My mother was very light-skinned and had red hair. I am sure these are qualities that endeared her to my dad.

When they decided to get married, my father's family did not accept his decision. My dad was the oldest in the family, and his decision was his decision. In fact, after they were married, his family was very upset and never spoke to me as his son.

I'm told that one day he walked into my grandmother's house, which would be his mother's house. In front of the family he announced that he had been down to City Hall and had adopted Ronald. His name now was Ronald Eugene Melvin. Dad's name was Albert Lee Melvin.

That became one of the secrets in my family. I did not know I was adopted. My mother and father had two more children together. My oldest sister was three years my junior. Being that she was my dad's first biological child, he loved her more than anything.

Don't get me wrong, my dad did not stop loving me; however, our relationship changed. He did have his favorite. He spoiled my sister to no end. Even as a child I developed feelings that I was second place.

I started to act up in many ways. Stealing money from my mother's pocketbook. Lying about anything for no reason at all. Stealing things from homes when I went to visit. This did not help endear me to my father. Why I stopped my negative behavior I don't know. I'm going to contribute it to the fact that I became what is known to be a Christian. I began to read the Bible, pray and go to church as often as possible. In fact, by the age of 16, I gave my first sermon.

My mother often spoke of how, for some reason, I had a 180° turn around. I am going to say it was because of my Christian involvement; however, being a young man, who is to say what it was. Dad and I never did grow close to each other. My sister was his favorite. And I had to understand that. From other stories in this book, I can prove the fact that he had unconditional love for me.

My father was big on demanding good behavior at the house. But that didn't go over too well with my sister. Because she was spoiled she thought she was boss. Who was I ever to tell her what to do? Of course, my mom and dad would always say, "Ronald, you take care of the girls." Then they would run off a list of things we were supposed to do. That did not set well with my older sister.

I must have been about sixteen or seventeen years old when a fight broke out between my sisters. I don't remember exactly what the fight was about, but my two sisters got into an altercation. It became physical.

My little sister could take care of herself, so she began to beat the devil out of my older sister. Hearing the ruckus, I went into the kitchen to see what was going on. My oldest sister grabbed a knife and was going after my younger sister.

I grabbed the knife and separated the two. My older sister was a very nasty person when she was upset. She turned to me and with bitterness said, "Don't touch me. You're not even my real brother." I noticed my younger sister looking shocked. I shook it off and did the best I could to get things back to normal again.

Soon after that situation, I happened to be sitting in the living room reading *Life* magazine. I remember it like it was yesterday. My mother came in and sat down on the opposite chair.

In my mind I envision her taking a book or magazine and beginning to read. Then she turned to me and said, "Ronald, I have something I have to tell you.

You are adopted. I am your mother, but your father adopted you and gave you his last name."

I don't know what my response was. If I remember well, I said okay and went on about my business. Now, having time to talk to my younger sister, I'm finding more details to the story.

It appears that she was being a busy body and looking through my parent's things in their home. She came across a small book. The book was my baby book my mother had started when I was born.

In the pages were details of how much I weighed, when and where I was born, my length, footprint, and my legal father's name. My sister, being quite intelligent for her age, understood right away what she had found.

Like all children she had to tell someone. And she shared it with my oldest sister. With that information my sister was armed and ready to unload. The altercation in the kitchen was just the right time to fire a weapon.

Albert Lee Melvin is my father. We did not see eye to eye for most of my life. But there was never a time I didn't think he loved me. I thought he was overbearing at times. I've learned that it helped keep me from making some terrible mistakes.

For example, if there was an event and trouble broke out, he would ask if I was there. If I said I was and explained I had seen what happened but I was not part of it, it didn't matter to Dad. If I was there it was as good as if I had been involved in whatever was happening.

You may find this a little over-the-top. Understand that I am a black male. I don't have the luxury of a second chance to explain the situation. The best way to handle a negative situation is not to be there at all.

My dad retired from the U.S. Customs. He had been so dedicated to his career that he and my mother had divorced by the time he retired. He was living in our old home by himself. I would go down and visit him. Many times, I would take my daughter with me. He treated her just like he treated my middle sister. She could do no wrong.

One day, I went to say hello to him. We sat out on the porch as he rocked back and forth as he usually did when he was sitting down. For some reason I turned to him and said, "I love you."

He never replied. I know he wanted to say he loved me. I love him even more now. I thank God each day for the love, shelter, protection and wisdom he gave me.

An evil lesson is soon learned. **English**

Life Lessons Begin

I miss the holidays when my mamma prepared a large meal for the extended family. Mamma would fill the table with an abundance that was fit for a king. Her menu included ham, turkey and sometimes a crown roast.

There would be snap beans, collards, mustard and turnip greens, corn pudding, macaroni and cheese, sweet potatoes with pineapple casserole, mashed potatoes, dressing and gravy, and homemade sweet rolls.

Everybody shared family stories with each other, with each person getting louder and louder so their voices could be heard. We children knew not to break into any of the adult's conversation. Of course, disagreements would break out. That's when I got quiet and listened for juicy stuff.

After the apple, sweet potato and lemon meringue pies, the coconut, devil foods, angel food and spice cakes were devoured, the young ones were sent outside. Occasionally I would re-enter the house. Voices would drop to a whisper. Sometimes the conversation would abruptly stop. Now and then they would forget I was in the house. This was my opportunity to hear one of those "not for children" family stories.

One story I overheard was about me. My parents were sharing an experience I had recently. This was an experience for which my parents had not prepared me.

I was in the sixth grade, eleven years old and was walking to school. Yes, I walked to school, uphill both ways. This was my first day at a new school, which was in a predominantly German community.

That morning, a block from the school, a white girl my age was standing in her doorway. From the steps she spit on me. That was followed by being called a nigger. I was too ashamed to tell my teacher.

Later that evening mom could sense that something was wrong. I told her of my first day at the new school. Mom took the time to comfort me. She explained that this was a very important lesson I needed to know, saying, "Not all grownups are nice. They tend to train their children the same way. It was not the little girl's fault. You are as good as anyone and don't forget it. Names do not define you, your actions do."

Aunt Margret interjected, "That little girl was lucky Ronnie was taught self-control."

"Lord, yes," replied Aunt Pearl. "Remember when he was in kindergarten? A classmate called him a nigger and he knocked him over a table." The room broke out in laughter.

The teacher had requested that my mother and she have a conference as opposed to suspending me. My mother was told I had to learn to control my temper.

My mother asked, "What happened? Ronald is not a physical child."

The teacher explained that one of my classmates had called me a name. I had become angry and hit the boy, knocking him over a couple desks.

Mom kindly asked what happened to the kid who called Ronald a name. The teacher said, "The child didn't know any better when he called him a nigger. Nothing happened, he knows better now."

Mom replied, "Then Ronald did the right thing, if there was no name-calling, there would be no hitting."

At home I was told to inform the teacher instead of hitting. After that incident Evelyn (my mother) never had to attend a parent-teacher's meeting at the school. As I got older I realized that name calling went both ways. Though I resented being called a name, I was just as guilty of the same thing. It's funny, when I was doing the name-calling I didn't see the harm. Mama straightened me out by the mistake of my little sister.

***One must eat first to be able to carry out religion.*
Vietnamese**

Grandma's Church

Between the ages of three and eight years old my parents sent me to spend the summers at my grandmother's home. My Grandmother Houston was a very special lady.

Mel with sister "Boppi" (Evelyn)

I believe this time with Grandmother Houston happened so my mother and father could have some personal time.

They didn't get any resistance from me. Grandmother's home smelled like love. She was always cooking. On Saturday evenings Grandmother would gather all the ingredients to make one of my favorites, her oven baked rolls, in preparation for Sunday's big dinner. I'd marvel at the way she added the ingredients for the rolls without measuring and then she would let the dough rise.

That was a miracle to me. After they had risen, she would break off little pieces of dough and line them up in a baking pan. In the morning the miracle would have happened again. The dough would have risen again to the perfect baking and eating size.
Yes, Sunday was very special. Sunday dinner could consist of one or even two of her many side dishes.

Whatever the side dishes were it never mattered to me. I was ready. Who could not love any or all of them, macaroni and cheese, collard and mustard greens, corn pudding, mashed potatoes and gravy, stewed tomatoes, corn on the cob, rice and gravy, string beans, sweet potatoes, kale, sweet peas, potato salad, macaroni salad, and sometimes succotash. No, I did not forget the rolls.

The meats were just as varied. Each large piece of meat always seemed to be something that had to be cooked slowly in the oven on low heat for a very long time. No one could roast chicken, ham, beef or pork like my grandmother.

Lord have mercy, for dessert grandmother would outdo herself. She made all types of fruit pies. When she fell a little short on time she would make a cobbler. Once in a while she would make a cake.

My favorite was a four-layer cake with jelly in between the layers. None of the food or desserts could be touched until after church. However, on the fourth Sunday the congregation brought to church a dish to be shared which meant we were eating at church that Sunday.

Actually, I thought grandmother lived in the church. You see, Monday night was prayer meeting, Tuesday night was Bible study, Wednesday night was the quilting bee, Thursday night was choir rehearsal and Friday we cleaned the church. On Saturday everybody went out and did all those things that would motivate them to go to church on Sunday.

Sunday morning started early, around 9:30, beginning with Sunday school, followed by an hour of prayer. This is when the congregation would get together and pray for all the sick, troubled, distraught, depressed, poor, the world in general and especially those who Satan had taken hold.

A deacon would start the prayer. He would then blend it into a prayer with a slow mournful sing-song cadence. The stronger the prayer the more the congregation would reply.

There would be many replies of "praise the Lawrd, God help us, oh Jesus, and Lawrd have mercy." I thought they would never stop. Just when I couldn't take it anymore, the deacon would begin to end the prayer service, which happened at about 10:30.

Now it was time for worship service. The church had an aisle down the middle. The deacons sat in the front rows on the left side of the church while the mothers of the church would sit on the right front. Each of the mothers wore all white. The only other one to wear white was the nurse, Miss Jenkins. These were the elders and leaders of the congregation and were the moral center of the church.

Every woman who entered the church had to have a hat. Not a little hat, a large hat. Each hat was decorated with flowers, feathers or fruit, and many had all the above.

I sat up in the front pew with grandmother. In fact, I sat between grandmother and my Aunt Virginia. Grandmother and Aunt Virginia were sisters who lived together. Sitting between them, I was so cute with my little legs shooting straight out.

In front of us was a raised staged area. On the left of the pulpit sat Deacon Edwards. Deacon Edwards was a senior deacon. He was an older conservative gentleman. On the right side sat Deacon Perry. Deacon Perry was a young up and coming deacon. Deacon Perry wore shark skin suits and two-tone shoes. His hair was processed.

During those days black men attempted to wear their hair like white men. It took a chemical process to straighten their hair. Therefore, it was called a "process." For those with money it was the look. For those without money it became a disaster. If you don't understand what I mean, look up pictures of past black entertainers like Sammy Davis Jr.

Each deacon sat in a large chair facing the congregation. The pastor of the church was Reverend Grace. His chair was much larger, sitting in the middle of the stage area. Reverend Grace would start his sermon by reading from the large Bible that sat on the lectern. Turning the pages of the Bible, Reverend Grace would share the scripture that would be the foundation of his sermon.

You knew when he had come to the end of the scripture and began to preach because he let out a grunt. It would go something like this: "And the Lord said unto Moses, grunt, go down Moses, grunt, into Egypt land, grunt, tell the Pharaoh, grunt, let my people go, grunt."

Have you ever visited a traditional Baptist church? Or more specifically, a black Southern Baptist church? If so, you know the congregation becomes part of the sermon.

Their spontaneous outbursts would motivate the pastor. Deacon Edwards would always reply with a "weeell." Now the sermon sounded like this: "And the Lord said, grunt, weeell, go down Moses, grunt, weeell, into Egypt land, grunt, weeell, tell the Pharaoh, grunt, weeell, let my people go grunt, weeell."

Sitting among the congregation was a lady by the name of Ms. Rose. Now everyone called Ms. Rose, including Grandma, big boned. I called her Ms. Rose. Repeating something like that could get me killed. Ms. Rose had a thing for Deacon Edwards. She wanted the deacon to know that she was in the audience. Ms. Rose would show her presence by replying to the deacon's "weeell" with a loud "ahmmmm."

We now had a three-piece band. The sermon sounded like this: "And the Lord said, grunt, weeell, ahmmmm. Go down Moses, grunt, weeell, ahmmmm. Into Egypt land, "grunt, weeell, ahmmmm. Tell the Pharaoh, grunt, weeell, ahmmmm. Let my people go grunt, weeell, ahmmmm."

You knew when Reverend Grace was really getting into his sermon. He began to pace back and forth on the pulpit. This particular Sunday things were going along fine until Reverend Grace went down on one knee.

This was not a good sign. This meant that we were in for a three-hour sermon. Normally, this would not be a problem. However, this happened to be the fourth Sunday.

On the fourth Sunday the sisters and mothers of the church would bring in their best dish. We would all go down to the church basement to share in the abundance of the Lord. That meant that the men in the church, including me, would have a taste of heaven. There would be plenty of fried chicken, potato salad, collard greens, cornbread, macaroni and cheese, and my personal favorite, sweet potato pie.

Deacon Perry was not having any of this. He was looking forward to planting his chair under a table of goodies that afternoon. That's when Deacon Perry went to his Plan B. He looked back to the choir director who was sitting at the piano.

She happened to be one of the church sisters with whom he had a relationship. He gave her a nod. She began to play quietly on the piano. This was a sign to the Reverend that it was time for him to bring his sermon to a close.

The Reverend started his closing but was still on one knee. Deacon Perry took his robe from the back of the Reverend's chair. He then draped the robe over Reverend Grace helping him up and leading him back to his chair.

If you have ever seen a James Brown review, you would have noticed a close resemblance to James Brown being led off the stage with a robe around his shoulders.

The choir stood and began to sing. In the choir was my mother and my Aunt Margaret. My mother was assigned to stand next to her. Aunt Margret stood at the end of a row. This way the only one next to her was my mother. This arrangement was very important.

You see, Aunt Margaret would get the Holy Ghost. For those of you not aware of what this is, it is when, during a sermon, one or more of the congregation starts to act erratically. These are members of the congregation who feel they have been touched by the hand of God. (There was a scene like this in the Blues Brothers movie.)

My Aunt Margaret took this to another level. She would fling her body and start swinging her arms all over the place. She had already put two people in the hospital and one was home recuperating. My mother was the only person who could stand beside her. Mama could avoid her because she knew how to bob and weave like a boxer. She was from the streets of Philadelphia.

When the choir got into the zone with a gospel favorite, Aunt Margaret got the spirit. She started wildly flinging her arms all over the place. Normally this wouldn't have been a problem.

Except that during the last week Mama had just gotten a new pair of dentures. She was in a world of hurt which made her forget about Aunt Margaret. She forgot to duck.

Aunt Margaret smacked her hard, right in the mouth. BAM! Those teeth went flying across the church. They ricocheted off a pillar and headed toward one of the stained-glass windows. Normally this wouldn't be a problem. You see, it just so happened that one of the glass pieces was missing.

On the previous Thursday there had been a funeral at the church. Mrs. Adam's husband had passed away. She had fourteen kids. Mrs. Adams came into the church throwing herself on the floor and kept screaming, "How am I going to feed the kids, how am I going to feed the kids, how am I going to feed the kids?" (She had the Holy Ghost.)

When they were able to get her to sit down, she continued screaming, hollering and kicking. Suddenly, one of her shoes flew off and went through the stained-glass window. Someone had duct taped a fan to cover the hole in the window. The space now read Hugh Die and Will Barry Funeral Home. I read it as You Die and Will Berry

Mama's dentures hit that taped fan dead in the center, slinging them back across the church and hitting Deacon Edwards right in the back of his head. BAM!

Deacon Edwards thought he had been touched by the hand of God. He leapt up and screamed WEEEEEELL!

Ms. Rose wasn't going to let that go unanswered. She leaped to her feet to answer him with a big AHMMMM!

To this day I don't know whether it was her blood sugar, the heavy jewelry, or the fur coat she was wearing. Then again, it could have been her powerful perfume. Whatever it was, it caused her to faint just as she stood up.

As she was falling she knocked the pew over backwards. Normally this wouldn't have been a problem except there was only one other person sitting on that bench and that was my Uncle Joe.

Uncle Joe was on a liquid diet. He didn't let anything pass his lips that wasn't a liquid of 80 proof or better. Weighing all of about ninety pounds, he was shot to the back of the church like a heat seeking missile.

Normally this wouldn't have been a problem. Except Sister Jenny, the church nurse, was taking a glass of water down to the front of the church to Aunt Virginia. Aunt Virginia had been touched by the spirit. She had thrown herself on the floor and was flopping around like a fish out of water.

Uncle Joe, on his way to the back of the church, hit Sister Jenny right at the knees. Uncle Joe took out Sister Jenny with a hit that would have made an all pro linebacker green with envy.

Sister Jenny hit that wall with such force that it rocked the front of the church. Grandmother thought the Lord was visiting the church. She leaped from the pew and threw her arms in the air, shouting, "Hallelujah!"

Normally this wouldn't have been a problem, except she forgot she was holding on to her walker and threw it in the air. It flew up towards the ceiling and became hooked on one of the blades of the ceiling fan. That walker was going around and around.

Not knowing where the walker was going, the congregation started to weave back and forth trying to avoid being hit by the flying walker. Reverend Grace, seeing the congregation moving back and forth, thought his sermon had touched the congregation like a powerful storm.

He was ready to give an encore. He leapt up from his chair, tripping over his robe. He began to roll forward across the pulpit and down into the congregation.

The congregation parted like the Red Sea. Reverend Grace came to a stop right in the middle of the church. He leapt to his feet and brushed himself off.

Looking around, he raised his hands up and with a loud voice said, "Praise the Lord, praise the Lord. Now pass the collection plate."

All wisdom is not taught in school. **Hawaiian**

The Wisdom of Grandma

My grandmother's values and wisdom laid the foundation for how I saw the world. I use Grandmother's wisdom to assist me in finding solutions. One of her most valuable lessons was that waiting and praying is only part of the formula.

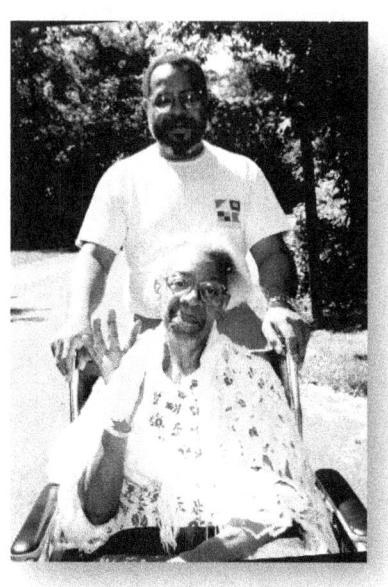

Grandmother and Mel

The other part is the responsibility of the individual to take initiative in solving a problem. Grandmother was an ordained minister. I was surprised when she shared this story about a minister who was looking for divine assistance, forgetting to help himself.

One night a minister's hometown was caught in a very bad hurricane. The waters began to rise. The minister realized the situation was quickly becoming desperate. He began to pray for divine intervention.

The city deployed buses throughout the communities to evacuate anyone who wanted to leave. When they arrived at the minister's home he refused to leave. He told them that the good Lord would provide for him. The bus left when he assured them that prayer would conquer all. The rain continued as did the rising of the water.

The height of the waters increased until only boats could circumvent the streets. The city government sent boats to evacuate anyone who was still in the neighborhoods. When they arrived at the minister's house he again insisted that they not worry. God would take care of him. The minister stood in water that was at his waist level. He knew the Lord would provide.

It began to rain harder. The water continued to rise. It was now at a very dangerous height. The water level was now at a level that the minister had to climb onto his roof.

Sitting on the roof in the downpour, a helicopter came by. They called down to him and told him to grab hold of the rope ladder. Again, he refused stating that the Lord would not let his prayers go unanswered. The waters continued to rise. The minister drowned.

The minster found himself at the golden gates of heaven. Entering the gates, he was well received. His family, friends and the congregation that preceded him welcomed him with open arms.

After the tour of the marvelous city of gold was finished, the newbies were asked if they had any questions or requests. "Yes," the minister said in his best sermon voice. Could he get an opportunity for an audience with the Lord? His request was promptly granted.

After exchanging pleasantries, the minister took this opportunity to ask the Lord something that was truly troubling him. Again, with his best authoritative voice he asked, "Lord I have always obeyed you. I have followed all your commandments and lived the life that was very close to being without sin. I taught your word faithfully and was a fisher of men and women. Why did you not save me from the storm?"

The Lord looked at him very sternly. The room became ungodly silent. With a booming voice the reply came, "I sent you a bus, a boat and a helicopter. What else would you expect of me?"

My grandmother was wise with age. Grandmother taught me lessons through story telling. Here's another I'll share with you. I wanted something very badly and I expected my parents to get it for me. They told me to earn the money by working. All I had to do was do some extra chores around the house. I was too lazy to do that. I felt I was owed.

My grandmother sat me down. She said boy (Grandmother could call me boy), "If you are starving you can ask God to provide you with food. God can have it cleaned and cooked, put in a bowl in front of you. If you do not grab a fork, pick it up, put it in your mouth, chew it up and swallow you will still die of starvation.

So, get off your fat butt, grab hold of the opportunity that is provided to get what you want. We all are given opportunities. What we do with those opportunities is truly up to us. Waiting around for the good Lord or someone to fix the problem is a perfect plan for failure. Don't forget the second part of that equation. You have to do something."

It's good to talk about troubles that are over.
Yiddish

Nobody Knows What Trouble I See

Palm Coast, Florida, has many amenities for the adult community. One of my favorites is its extensive adult education program. Being curious and wanting to try something new and different, I registered for a class titled Spiritual Journey.

I enjoyed the class immensely. The focus of study was personal spiritual growth. I enrolled in this class due to its focus on personal spiritualism as opposed to religion.

During one session a classmate seemed to be struggling. She shared that she had just lost her husband. They had been quite close. She had gotten cancer and her husband had been her moral support. He was there to comfort her through chemotherapy and she was a cancer survivor. Then he was diagnosed with cancer and passed quickly.

She questioned why she was still alive. How is it that her husband was dead and instead of her? The class tried to console her. She wanted to know when the pain would go away. Does the pain ever stop?

The room became silent for what seemed like hours. Without thinking, I spoke up. I told her I didn't believe that the pain ever goes away. You learn to live with it more each day.

Then from out of nowhere some unknown trigger will be pulled. Memories will be woken and take over your emotions. You will be reintroduced to your pain. I had a reason for being so sympathetic. I too carried a similar pain.

Sometime ago several friends and I were having a few beers and a snack. The group began to tease each other about their birthdays. I tried to avoid this conversation.

Unlike most people I don't enjoy my birthday. My birthday was later that month. This was the month I lost two boys in a fire. One was four and the other seven years old.

I had pushed it to the back of my mind for personal survival. I've forgotten the date. What I remember is it was the late 70's, the month of March.

I had celebrated my birthday with a house party that week. The two boys, Kathy and I had just returned home from a full day of shopping. I was hoping for an early spring. No luck - it was quite blustery in the city of Philadelphia.

The two boys proceeded upstairs to prepare for bed. Kathy and I emptied the bags while the boys changed their clothing. We were all tired that evening. My recollection is that Kathy and I prepared to go to bed the same time as the boys.

I woke up to the sound of sirens. They sounded very close. That is expected when you live in the city. The flashing red lights aroused my attention. I leapt from the bed and went directly to the window. Through the window I could see a large fire truck in front of the home.

If you're not familiar with the city of Philadelphia, it is like most East Coast cities. There are blocks and blocks of row homes on small streets. Cars can only park on one side of the street. Today when they build similar multiple homes side by side, they are called townhouses.

We lived on a very narrow street. It must've been one of the early streets of Philadelphia. Parking on one side of the street allowed only enough room for one vehicle to use the street.

The fire engine apparently had to ride partially on one side of the pavement to fit in the street. It was gigantic. Its bright lights were flashing red and blue, lighting up the small street.

Being concerned and not knowing what, if anything, was wrong, I woke Kathy, who went and woke up the boys sleeping in the adjoining room. Returning to the window, I looked for evidence of the commotion.

In my mind's eye, I remember how sleepy the boys looked. They were both rubbing their eyes in the confusion. Still not able to comprehend the situation I decided to prepare to leave the house. This was the middle of the night and it had gotten colder.

Kathy decided that the boys needed to get a coat or jacket just in case we had to leave the house. Obeying, the boys turned and went back to their room. That would be the last time we were together as a family.

Back at the window I opened it to better assess the situation outside. The environment had changed. The radios were squawking loudly. Additional fire trucks, sirens and flashing lights were clogging the street. I opened the window and looked down.

I observed firemen rushing around below. Through all the noise of the radios and the sirens I heard one of the firemen yell, "There are people in that house!"

Unexpectedly I heard a loud crash. I believe it was the firemen breaking through the front door. I turned around and the lights shut off. I could see only the flashing lights from the emergency vehicles.

Smoke rushed into the room choking both of us. Kathy began to lose consciousness. I grabbed her and started towards the bedroom to get the boys. Approaching the stairwell, the intense heat drove us back.

Looking down the stairwell, the fire had consumed the bottom of the steps, the down stairs glowed and wiggled from the heat. Realizing we could not exit that way, I half dragged Kathy back to the front bed room, coughing and feeling my way.

We had to get out as soon as possible. The smoke was so great I could no longer see at all.

Kathy lost consciousness as I was pulling her toward the window. Choking, I supported her body so she could get air from outside. The firemen put up a ladder to the window and the first fireman entered the room. Kathy had begun to recover.

The fireman, speaking through his breathing apparatus, told me to help Kathy onto the ladder. We helped her out the window onto the ladder. Turning to me, he directed me to descend the ladder.

I proceeded to run to get the boys. The firemen grabbed me. Through his mask he asked me where I was going. I explained to them I had two boys. They had gone to get more clothing from their bedroom and had not returned. I was not leaving without the boys. The firemen said that he could not let me stay in the building. I had to leave. Then he would go get the boys.

This would not happen until I left the house. I had no choice. I could stay and argue wasting time or allow him to save the boys. Frustrated, I exited through the window by the ladder, leaving the fireman and trusting he would save the boys. Shaking, I swung myself onto the ladder descending to the street.

By this time, the neighbors were out and attempting to assist in any way possible. One family took Kathy into their home. I sat on the curb with nothing on but a shirt and pants. It had to be in the lower 20's. I felt nothing.

The more I sat, the stronger the stress. My concern for the boys was escalating. I kept asking, "What about the boys?"

Instead of answering the firemen would respond with a question: "How old were they? Where were they in the house? Were they together?" They wouldn't let me near the house.

Without warning the house seemed to explode. I know now this is what is called flashback. The flash was quick and bright like a camera flash. I remember a fireman falling out of the house at that point. He seemed to be shot out of the house. I knew the boys were gone. My body went weak after that. I gave up.

I realized I was very cold. I watched the firemen bringing out two stretchers. On each was a body bag. I was restrained and not allowed to go near them.

Locating the neighbor's house where Kathy had taken shelter, I took her to her mother's home. I stayed for a while, then left. I needed to be by myself. I went to my parent's home. I don't remember much more about that night or the following days, except how happy my mother was of my survival.

In the next couple of days, we were in a daze. We had to attend to funeral preparations. I don't remember the funerals or much of the burial.

I remember very clearly the Catholic Church refusing any burial in the Catholic cemetery until Kathy went through some act of attrition. That irritated me to no end. I'm from a Southern Baptist background. I thought, how could someone, especially the church, be so thoughtless and cruel?

That anger and pain stains my memory. I've tried to distance myself from the event. My relationship with their mother fell apart quickly in the following months. We both handled our grief in different ways.

Were we blaming ourselves or each other? Today we are good friends. There is still a lot of internal pain. Pain still sneaks up on me any day, any time. I am especially sensitive around my birthday.

The pain will forever be a part of my life. Like the lyrics of an old Glen Campbell song 'The winds of memory flow though the inner corridors of my mind.' When someone wishes me happy birthday, it is a reminder of the loss of two young boys. Two boys who would be men today.

Five years ago, I was teaching a management class. During the class there was a video referencing the plane bombing in Ireland. Several of the interviewees shared their loss of a family member. Out of nowhere the memories rushed into my mind. I was caught so off guard I had to leave the room to compose myself.

Yes, you learn to live with the pain each day. No, it never goes way.

Stupidity does not tolerate wisdom. **African (Ovambo)**

Famous Last Words: 'Watch This'

Have you ever been in a situation when someone says, "Watch this?" That's when you know something is going to go wrong.

Each year my family would go visit relatives in New Jersey. Family and friends looked forward to this annual event, where we gathered on the farm owned by one of the family members.

The women gathered together in the house, with the young children. They were on a mission: cooking and sharing stories. The men spent most of the day skeet and trap shooting. Later, the men joined the ladies and after a few drinks, the voices grew louder, and the stories grew wilder.

We older children, about eight or nine of us, were left to roam the farm. How much trouble could we find? Right, we were kids. Lance, the oldest of our group, was fourteen. He was in charge. The rest of us ranged between seven and ten.

Off we went. Just the guys, no girls allowed. We walked through the cornfield. We visited the barn. We took off to explore wherever adventure led us. At some point we came across an electrified fence. We had been warned about the fence. Lance started to challenge us to touch it.

"You touch it."

"No, you touch it."

"I'm not touching it."

Each one of us challenged the other to touch the fence. None of us was stupid enough to do so. During the argument we heard Lance holler, "Watch this!"

When I turned around, Lance had found a tree stump close to the fence. He was standing on the stump. He had proceeded to urinate over the fence. We were all impressed with the power and the grace of the arc. Each of us was awed with his bravery.

Like all things, what goes up must come down. Lance's stream started to lose its power. Ever so slowly the ark closed. Then there was a loud 'pop!' sound.

Lance's stream had hit the electrified fence. The noise surprised all of us. When my eyes cleared, we looked around for Lance. We had heard him scream.

Lance was lying on the ground with his hands covering his crotch. A little stream of smoke was coming from his zipper. He was screaming for his mother. Instead of us running to his aid, we thought it was the funniest thing we had ever seen. We were laughing and crying so hard, we were unable to go get our parents.

The adults must've heard the commotion. They came to investigate. There was Lance on the ground, crying and holding his crotch.

For the next week or so Lance's crotch was bandaged. It had to be more than a week before the swelling went down.

When a father gives to his son, they both laugh; when the son gives to his father, they both cry. **Yiddish**

Lessons of the Father

My father was a stern, fair, conservative man. He was a born leader and was a sergeant during WWII. Dad was also a leader in the community. While serving in the Army he was a golden gloves boxing champion.

Cheryl (Cookie), Evelyn (Boppi) and Ronald (Mystic Mel)

He stood over 6'6", weighing over 250. His voice was deep and booming. You could hear him over anyone in any situation. He applauded with the same intensity. His clapping could be heard above the crowd, no matter how large.

Dad enjoyed completing the *Philadelphia Inquirer* crossword puzzle. He claimed it kept his mind sharp. Dad was one of, if not the first, black customs officer in the United States. Like with all things, Dad took his job responsibilities very seriously.

As a customs officer in the U.S. Treasury Department he was extremely dedicated and earnest. Most of the neighbors were unaware of his occupation. During his early years as a customs officer he only wore his uniform on the job. He would never wear that uniform out of the house.

Each day he left for work with his uniform in a garment bag. He would change into his uniform when he got on location. Dad polished his shoes each evening. When he left the house, his shoes were so shiny it was possible to use them as mirrors. One of the things I remember was Dad training me to shine my shoes.

Dad had high standards for me. He expected me to meet or surpass them. This became the catalyst of our many clashes. I was a nerd. Electronics were my friend. Dad measured me by all things physical.

I was not only expected to have high academic grades, he expected me to be physically strong and well groomed. There I was 5'5" weighing about 145 pounds. I found it difficult to meet my father's expectations of being both academically and physically strong.

While my friends were outside playing, I had to sit and practice my writing. Making circles repeatedly. Then making up and down strokes as though I was making lower case cursive W's. There I sat repeating these movements over and over again. I was perfecting each movement so I could produce perfect letters. I still hate writing.

Realizing I could never meet his expectations, I stopped trying. Then the war began. Each task became a battle. I didn't clean up after the dog correctly. I didn't set the trash at the curb correctly. I didn't do my homework correctly.

When I tried to learn to write like him, my handwriting was too fancy. However, his handwriting was so fancy he could have signed the Declaration of Independence! It was only as an adult I learned how much he loved me.

Evelyn, my princess sister, could do no wrong. Truthfully, she was quite intelligent. Until the day she died she was able to name each student in her classes back to kindergarten. Without even opening the textbook most of the time, she was able to accomplish getting A's in all her subjects.

Cookie, my baby sister, and I became good friends. We are still very close friends today. We both have a weird sense of humor and we love telling stories to each other over the phone. Cookie would accompany me and my friends when we went roller skating. She became one of the guys.

I was about seventeen when I found out why my oldest sister, Evelyn, was the apple of Dad's eye. It was then that I found out that I had been adopted. The gene pool between my sister and I were different. There was no way I could meet my father's physical expectations. In addition, I had dyslexia.

During those times students were not tested for dyslexia. Dad had the same high academic expectations for all of us. I was the lowest academic achiever in the family. Both of my sisters excelled in school.

In time of test, the family is best. **Burmese**

Dad's Brothers, Tom and Leroy

The aspirations for strength and physical abilities ran deep in Dad's family. I remember one time his brothers came to visit. Both brothers were members of the 101st Airborne Division. They were part of the first blacks accepted as paratroopers.

Their uniforms were immaculate. Their pants bloomed around their large high, black, shiny boots. They looked like gods to me, being every bit as big as my father. Each had a chest full of metals and decorations.

Did I mention that their boots had a mirror finish just like Dad's? They seemed to be fond of me for some reason. Then they started to toss me around like a football. It scared the hell out of me.

Why is that memory so strong? They began to challenge each other as brothers will do. At one challenge they attempted to lift the rear of a car. Trust me, they were able to lift that car. That gives you some idea of the athletic ability that was expected of me.

It is better to live in a good neighborhood than to be known afar. **Norwegian**

Talking about the Ghetto

The neighborhood began to change quickly. My Irish friends and families moved to other parts of the city. I have never been able to contact them, nor have they tried to contact me. Occasionally, I'd see them on American Bandstand with Dick Clark. The broadcast studio was just a couple of miles from my home. Blacks were not allowed on the show.

As the neighborhood changed, Dad tightened his rein on me. In those days we went to neighborhood schools. I attended two of the local schools. Dad would walk the distance to each school and back again. He noted the time it took to walk the distance and allowed me five minutes on either side.

If I was not home within five minutes, I had to account for my whereabouts and answer why it took me so long getting home.

Don't do the crime, if you can't do the time.

Arriving home from school one day I found my father sitting on the porch, smoking a cigarette. I must've been around ten years old. He had been waiting for me. I was pulled sternly into the house. By this time in our relationship, I was in almost total fear of my father.

He started questioning me. The scene was very similar to a law enforcement movie. He was questioning me like someone accused of a crime.

The questions came quickly. What time did I leave school? Was I with anyone? Did you stop at any place along the way? Did I know a girl by the name of Pat?

One question after another was met with a reply of yes or no. Each answer was followed by "Sir." I replied, "Yes, I came directly from school, no, there was no one with me, no, I did not stop anywhere and no, I did not know any girl by the name of Pat."

He told me that I had better not be lying to him. If I was, I was in very serious trouble. With that he told me to get my hat and coat and follow him.

We walked down about two blocks from our home. Dad stopped at a house and rung the bell. A lady answered the door. Dad explained to her that we were the number she had called.

This lady was unknown to me. I was asked if I knew her daughter. I replied, "No sir." Her daughter and I attended the same school.

Dad had me write down my phone number. It was checked with a piece of paper sitting on the table. "You should be very happy," my father said. "These two hand writings do not match."

The gist of the story was that someone had broken into the house. The thieves took some pieces of jewelry, but the worst part was the flour and sugar that was thrown all over the kitchen. Nothing else was stolen.

The lady pointed to the pad on the counter top that had our phone number on it. Dad had me write my phone number to see if the writing matched. I had been trying to write like him, so my numbers were very fancy. My four had a loop in the corner. This proved I was not the writer of the note.

Dad, being a law enforcement officer, was quite familiar with investigating a crime. How he figured out who wrote that number, I don't remember. I do remember that he was able to figure out who and where they lived.

He did this right there in our kitchen. Somehow, he had followed the evidence to their apartment. She had two daughters and they had broken into the house.

The oldest daughter had a crush on me. I was totally oblivious to any of this! She had used the phone book to find my number and she wrote it down. Then she tried to call me. I was cleared of any wrong doing when they found the jewelry at their house.

Dad never apologized to me. His remarks were, "You should be grateful that you were not involved."

By the time I attended high school the neighborhood had totally changed. Communities like mine were known as ghettos. Known for poor black folk that had no desire to achieve. That was far from the truth. Most were there due to the circumstance of being black.

Though many of the families were financially capable of buying homes in another area of Philadelphia, the banks would only finance homes for blacks in certain neighborhoods. The homes never appreciated in value. In fact, the homes decreased in value. Then the houses would be bought out; gentrification would push the black families away.

Each home was being sold for a fraction of its original cost. There goes the neighborhood. Those moving in had a significant supply of resources. A new upscale community was created. When you can't control your community, you cannot control your life style.

Gangs invaded the neighborhood. The mothers used to watch us from out of their windows as we walked to and from school. Because of gang activity, they abandoned their posts for their own safety. Whether or not it was fear, I'm only guessing.

Each neighborhood gang started a draft. If you lived within a gang's boundaries you became part of that gang. This mimicked a sports draft. However, unlike a sports draft, if you didn't join you were subject to beatings, harassment or both. Gangs took on names based on their location. My neighborhood gang was called Eighth and Norris after a street corner. Owning the corner was similar to a clubhouse or headquarters.

Over the years my dad had been promoted several times. His shift was still in constant rotation. Most of the time when he was sleeping, I was at home trying to be quiet. Who was going to wake my dad for dinner was a fear my siblings and I had. What was so unnerving about this task? Dad never woke up in a pleasant mood. It was better if you were not the first one to be seen.

I worked hard at making myself scarce. Most of the time when he was awake, I was either at school or at a school activity. If he caught me at home, we would sit and I would get an instructional sermon.

There were only three sermons that I remember. First was about sex, the second was etiquette when being stopped by the police, and the third was staying out of the gangs. He explained to me that the gangs were infiltrating the community. There was only one option when it came to gang activity. I was not to associate or be part of the gang activity. If he found out I disobeyed his wishes, he felt obligated to kill me. I totally believed him. My father was a man of his word. Trust me on this.

My friends joined the gang. There were about nine of them from within a block of my house. Josh was the gang's warlord. Joshua's family's backyard and mine backed up to each other. During these early times of gangs, guns were scarce in the gang culture.

Joshua stopped me several times and confronted me about being part of the gang. I told him in no uncertain words that was I not going to join the gang. Both my father and Josh claimed they would kill me. My father or the gang could kill me. I knew for sure my father would.

Coming home from school one day, I turned the corner to my house. Josh and a large group of boys, which included some of my friends, were standing around the entrance to my home. I pushed my way past them and went into the house. It was unusual to find my father sitting on the sofa reading a book.

I asked him how he was doing. And he grunted an okay and that was the end of our conversation. I changed out of my school clothes then looked out the window. The group had not left. I began my homework. My father called me into the living room asking why I wasn't outside with my friends. I explained that I had a lot of homework.

Dad knew I hated homework. He was aware that I would procrastinate till the last moment. Getting up from the sofa he walked to the window. Looking outside he saw the group of boys. Turning to me he asked if they were my friends.

I acknowledged that they were. He then asked why I wasn't going outside. Again, I explained that I had homework to do. Asking me if I had my house key I said yes. He asked for it.

I took the lanyard from around my neck. My key was attached so it wouldn't get lost. After handing the key to him he walked me to the door and pushed me out.

My father had many taboos for me. Near the top of the list was no boxing. My guess is because he was a Golden Glove boxing champion, he was very reluctant to see me take that route. Up until that point he had given me some instruction, but I was never to use it unless physically threatened.

I guess if he couldn't box, I couldn't box. My mother, being brought up in a religious home, hated boxing. She hated violence of any kind. He had given up boxing because of my mother's wishes.

I was grabbed and pulled into the center of the group. That day I fought and fought and fought. Boy, I really got beaten up. In my defense, I had delivered some good swings of my own. Everybody went home. I went in the house and cleaned up as if nothing had ever happened. My father and I never spoke of that event.

This story helps explain why we didn't get along. Today I doubt if I'm as wise as he was then. I'm sure I wouldn't be able to handle the same situation with his understanding.

Now that I am grown, I understand that Dad knew about handling a gang situation. Dad was also aware of the gang looking for me. If they had caught me away from my home they might have seriously hurt, if not killed, me. Being able to observe the event in front of the house, he was able to step in at any time and bring it to a halt.

From that day on I was never asked about joining the gang. Later, I watched as one by one, each of my friends dropped out of the gang.

Don't join in a fight if you have no weapons.
African (Swahili)

Josh

Remember Josh (The Ghetto)? Josh was the leader of the group that had confronted me in front of my house. Josh was known to be the gang warlord. That meant he had to be the meanest member in the group. If there were weapons, he had control of them.

I don't remember how and when it happened, but Josh and I became friends. I was dedicated to the church at that time, attending as often as possible. On a whim I invited Josh to join me. Dropping out of the gang, Josh began to attend church with me.

I had a job washing dishes at the local hospital. They needed another washer and I asked Josh if he wanted the job. Josh took the job and did well.

I had to stop working for a while to play football. Josh did so well he was promoted. He met a young lady and they made plans to get married. My memory is not quite clear about what happened next. I graduated from high school and went on to start my career. Things did not go well with Josh. My lifestyle did not allow us to spend a lot of time together.

When I bumped into him, he just didn't seem the same. I finally realized that he was on drugs. Not knowing what to do, I began to avoid him. If you knew my father, you understood why I had to stay clear of Josh.

The last time I saw Josh he was laying in the doorway of an old vacant store. I said hello and asked if there was something I could do for him. He looked at me and said his mother had thrown him out of the house. Then he asked me for money.

I knew if I gave it to him, Josh would buy more drugs. I found a way to avoid giving him the money. We talked for a while, then he nodded off. I continued home and never saw him again. I found out from his brother that he had died from a drug overdose.

I often wonder if I correctly handled the situation.

Learning cannot be inherited. **Yiddish**

Lesson Learned

Everyone and anyone growing up in Philadelphia around the 50s, 60s or 70's knows that boxing was king. When I was in high school Sonny Liston was the heavyweight world champion. He lived and trained in Philly.

Mohammad Ali took his title. He also trained in Philly. Then there was Smoking Joe Frazier who lived and trained in Philly. Each fighter held the heavy weight title at one time or another. Did I mention Rocky Balboa is based on a fighter from Philadelphia?

On Fridays, Dad watched the Cavalcade of Sports which was Friday night boxing. This was his Monday night football. On Sunday mornings there was a TV program with children around the ages of ten to thirteen boxing. It was called the "Sweet Sport."

I boxed whenever I could. No, not in the ring boxing. Our boxing was performed on the street corner under the street lights. We sparred with open hands. I believe we called it shadowboxing. Dad was against me being involved in this activity.

Twice I was caught shadow boxing on the corner. Dad laid down the law each time. The third time he caught me, he challenged me. If you want to box, he said, I had to box him. It just so happened that this was right in front of my house.

My friends stood around startled that I would box my father. Mom heard the commotion and came to the door. I put my hands up and began my young boy bobbing, weaving and fake jabs. I was only 5'5." That didn't bother me. I was young and quick. Being over six-foot-tall all Dad had to do was to hold his arms straight out.

There was no way I could reach him. He held one hand on my forehead. The other hand was in front of my face. Not only could I not see, my arms were too short to reach him. This resembled a scene from a cartoon. The large guy holds his arm out placing it on the forehead of his opponent. The little guy keeps swinging but finds it impossible to reach the larger guy.

Dad kept his left hand stretched out. I kept trying to get under it. Every now and then Dad would push me away just because he could. What happened next, I would never forget. He had enough of my foolery.

Dad took the heel of his right arm off my forehead. Then it was over. Dad hit me right under my nose with the flat of his hand.

I almost blacked out, my nose began to bleed, and my knees became weak. Worst of all my mother screamed. Running down the steps she kept screaming, "My baby, my baby" over and over again. She rushed over grabbing me and led me into the house.

For weeks after that when my friends saw me, they would all breakout with, "My baby, my baby," laughing as hard as they could.

That was the end of my boxing career.

The whole village is mother to the motherless.
Indian (Tamil)

The Village

Back in the day, the black community was truly a village. The stay-at-home moms were watchful of the children. From the windows the mothers observed the children as they traveled to and from school. If you attempted to step out of line, chances are that one or more of the moms would be watching.

As a child I thought I was smarter than adults. Now, that I'm an adult I wonder why we kids were so naive. For instance, there was this one occasion where I thought I would not be caught. No one would see me.

What I did has been lost in time. I have no idea of what my sin was. All I know is one of those nosy, sneaky mothers somehow had seen me. Before I knew what was happening, one of the mothers grabbed and spanked me. The telephone was not my friend.

When I arrived home, mom knew all about it. I was spanked again. Then came the ultimate disaster. Mom said, "Wait until your father gets home." Dad, on his arrival home, announced he would take care of it after dinner. At the dinner table I sat, not being able to eat. A huge lump in my throat prevented me from swallowing.

Today, many would say this is child abuse. We were not abused by our parents. Parents loved and respected their children. I was a quick learner. All it took was one or two spankings before I got the idea.

There were times I could feel eyes on me. Turning around and seeing that stern face, I knew it was time to step away from whatever I was doing. Our family and the community had high expectations of moral values. The community held you accountable.

Now that I think about it, we were blessed.

A good man is a man of goods. **(Unknown)**

Great Expectations

Many men balk at marrying a woman with children. This is more strongly believed of black men. My community has a bad reputation when it comes to fathers being responsible. That is truly a myth.

I was born before my mother met and married Dad. This was at the end of WWII. Dad returned home, falling in love with a single parent, my mother. Dad stood well over 6 foot tall. He had been a Golden Glove champion in the Army.

He had risen to the rank of Sergeant. I am sure my father had plenty of opportunities to meet someone who did not have "baggage." This action is evidence to me of how much my father loved my mother and me. It takes a real man to adopt, giving his last name to someone else's child. This was the value system I learned to live by.

The same expectations that Dad had for himself, he expected of me. There was a major problem. Dad was a large man, athletic, and he expected me to follow in his footsteps. Trying to play sports like him was difficult at best. I stood a little over five foot five. The pressure caused me to do whatever I could to man up. I began body building, weight training, swimming and playing football.

In real life I was a first-generation geek. Electronics was my first love. I worked hard for money to buy electronic equipment. I built my tuner, pre-amp, speakers and amplifiers. I learned to program on my Apple II. Later I built my own computers.

Not being an avid sports fan or capable player, Dad and I grew apart from each other. I knew he cared for me. He had high expectations for me becoming a college athlete.

This was not to be in my future. I was an average athlete and a poor student. His disappointment became evident in our relationship, or lack of a relationship. I pushed myself to meet his expectations. Failing so many times, I gave up.

By the time I was in my late twenties, Dad had retired from the Treasury Department. He and my mother were divorced and he was living by himself. I made every effort to see him once a week. From our conversations, I realized he loved me. It was during that time I told him I loved him. He never responded because Dad saying he loved me, or anyone, was out of the question.

It is folly to fear what one cannot avoid. **Danish**

Dad, the Coach and Mel
The Unholy Three

Dad stood 6'6" weighing over 250 pounds. Dad had been a Golden Glove boxing champion. He had a commanding presence, with a voice very loud and very low. He instilled fear in me all my life. My fear was that he could and would kill me at any time.

Whenever I was getting close to the dark side he let me know that at any time I could cease to exist. That was enough for me. I was bent on self-preservation. There were times I could feel him watching me even from across the room.

Unknown to him or mother, I had a learning disability, dyslexia. At the time I attended school, students were not tested for disabilities. If you needed glasses, for example, it was not discovered until a child was in the fourth or fifth grade.

Even though dad expected good grades, he also expected me to play in sports. I had to play football.

Me, I loved football. The problem was I stood about 5'5" and weighed about 145 pounds. I walked to school each day approximately four miles, doing this because I also had asthma. The walking helped me with endurance so I could play football.

Between asthma, allergies and my size, I was not going to survive training. I had to do something. During the off-season I became a body builder and swimmer. Being small, I was quick. Being muscular, I became a human fire hydrant.

Playing defense, I was a mean tackler. Dad gave me a secret weapon, teaching me to watch the ball carrier's feet, no matter how he moved with his shoulders or where he looked. The runner had to go where his feet went. I focused on their feet. Rarely did I miss a tackle.

The coach enjoyed my enthusiasm and my willingness to put my body in jeopardy. Dad only came to one game since his work schedule fluctuated, making it difficult for him to be available during afternoon matches.

This was the first and last time dad would see me play. Knowing he was there I wanted to show him my skills. I began to show off a little bit. One of my teammates got into a shoving match with one of the opposing players. I jumped in and pushed the player away from my teammate. The referee almost threw me out of the game. My father saw the whole thing.

As I approached the bench Dad pulled me to the side. He read me the riot act about being a good team player and sportsman. At that point the coach came over to question who the hell he was. I introduced him as my father.

The coach looked at me and then he looked at my father. Actually, he looked down at me and up at my father. I will never forget him taking a second look. Then he said, "Hell, the milkman must've been your father."

I knew the coach was going to die. There was the possibility that we might've been cleaning the coach up off the field. Fortunately, Dad had a good sense of humor.

Dad shared with the coach that I was his adopted son.

Children do not understand the hearts of parents.
(Japanese)

Channeling Mom and Dad

My family and extended family have drifted apart. The passing of family members exacerbates the situation which has resulted in the elimination of family get-togethers. Reminiscing on those days, I lament the loss of my family's fellowship. The food, the stories and the love.

Mel and Ronnie

If there is anything I regret it is not being the glue that holds my family and extended family together.

Remember that old Frank Sinatra recording "My Way?" In the recording Frank shares these lyrics,

"Regrets, I've had a few, but then again, too few to mention." That's me. One of my regrets is being an absentee father to both my two daughters. I love my daughters. They have grown to be strong, independent and beautiful.

I hope that they would agree that I tried to spend time with them as often as possible. There must be one or two adventures with me that they could share. Not having a lot of time with them, I had few opportunities to be a real parent. There is one time that stands out.

My oldest daughter lived a good distance from my home. I would not see her for weeks, months and later for years. Ronnie was around the age of 13 when she ran away from home.

I had not expected a phone call from Ronnie. When I answered the phone, I knew she was in distress. We began to talk. It was then I found out she wanted to come live with me. For me that would've been a blessing. I missed her so very much.

Ronnie asked me if I would pick her up. Of course, I would. However, I did not know the location of where she was staying with her mother. Ronnie told me not to worry she was at the shopping mall.

"You're at the mall?"

"Yes," she said.

"Why are you at the shopping mall?" I questioned. "How did you get there?"

That is when she informed me that she had ran away from home. She had ridden her bike to the mall. I began to panic. She was out all by herself on a bike. Finding out her exact location, I quickly drove to the shopping mall.

We sat down at one of the restaurants to talk. Ronnie was crying heavily. She shared the story that she and her mother had had an argument. Therefore, she did not want to stay there anymore.

They were not treating her with love and respect. She requested if she could come live with me. "Of course," I said. "We first have to share this with your mother."

Ronnie was adamant that she did not want to go back to the house. I explained that legally I could not take her with me without her mother being informed.

This is where it began to hurt. My child was in pain and I did not want her to go back to the place where the pain began. Even so, I realized there would be more pain for both of us if we did not handle this correctly.

I convinced Ronnie that if nothing else, we had to get her clothes. Here was the plan. We would go back to the house together. She would tell her mother the decision she had made, that she wanted to come to live with me. I was going to agree. We would collect her things and I would take her home with me.

It was a silent ride back to her home. Arriving at her house, we all sat down to discuss the situation. This included Ron's stepfather.

Ron explained that she had decided to come live with me. Ronnie's mother asked me if I knew why she had ran away. I told her no, I didn't know. All I knew was that she was unhappy living there. That was more than enough for me.

Ronnie's mother began to explain that this all came about because of Ronnie's report card. "What report card?" I asked. It seems that Ronnie had not received very good grades the ending of that school year. Ronnie, thinking she was smarter than the average parent, had changed the grades and signed her mother's name.

I asked Ronnie if that was true. She acknowledged that her mother was correct. She didn't see why she had to be punished for her transgressions.

The pain hit deep, and my mind began to twirl. I was caught behind the eight-ball. There was going to be pain no matter what I did. What would Mom do? What would Dad expect of me? Sharing this now, the emotions returning make me uncomfortable.

What would Dad expect of me? How would Mom handle this? Time to put on my big boy pants. Do what you believe your mother would do.

"Ronnie, I'd love to have you come live with me. But first, you have some business you must deal with. Then you can change households. What you did was wrong. Your mother has every right to be upset. You must deal with your mother. After that is done, if you would like to come live with me you'd be welcomed. You know how to contact me. I'll be waiting with open arms for your call."

I strolled over and gave her a hug and a kiss. I walked out the door. The pain was sharp, the tears flowed. What would my daughter think of me?

Dad would be proud of me. It was not easy. I was unsure of what my daughter thought of me. We did not have contact for some time.

I know now that was what my father would have expected of me. His training had toughened me up for situations like this.

Ronnie and I are like peas in a pod now. All we need is to hear each other's voice and we began to laugh. How did that come about? My son-in-law. That's another story from behind the eight-ball.

Love your friend with his faults. **Italian**

Bruce

I am addicted to motorcycles. I love to look at them. I love to ride them. I love to hear them. It should come as no surprise to anyone who knows me about my excitement when Bike Week and Biketoberfest comes to Daytona Beach. During this time there could be up to a quarter of a million bikers enjoying our beaches.

Bruce Wynne

There are many venues spread out between Jacksonville and Orlando. The epicenter is in Daytona Beach. Bike Week and Biketoberfest draws people from around the world. Having so many potential customers in one place, the manufacturers of motorcycles, motorcycle clothing and accessories migrate here each year for these two events.

The Speedway, which is the NASCAR Daytona Speedway, becomes a hub of activity. Manufacturers of motorcycles stake out their territory to show and demonstrate their product to you.

Surrounding them are all the trappings that one needs to become a motorcyclist. For example, you can find anything from the bike itself, to the clothes, to accessories, any part you want or need including motors, radios, specialty oil, exhaust pipes, patches, air painting, tires and plenty of beer.

I ride a Kawasaki Voyager. This is a large motorcycle resembling a Honda Gold Wing. Kawasaki has its own area around the speedway. I would visit there at least two or three times during Bike Week.

They would have coffee and snacks available while you looked at the new motorcycles. Not only could you look, but if a bike was available you could go for a ride with one of their guys. This gave me the opportunity to try several of their bikes.

I was having a cup coffee one morning in the Kawasaki tent when several riders came and sat at the table with me. At least one or two of them were also riding Kawasaki Voyagers. They asked me where I had my bike maintained.

I explained that I did not have anyone special and was always looking for a good mechanic. They shared with me that they had a neighbor who lived in Palm Coast, not far from where I lived. He was not only an excellent mechanic, but he had also been a competitive rider earlier in his life. They suggested that I give him a call and gave me his number.

Bike Week was over and I parked my bike. Outside of Bike Week I only rode one or two times during the week. One evening I received a call and a gentleman introduced himself as Bruce.

He explained that some friends of his had been to the Kawasaki pavilion. They were the same ones that I had met during Bike Week. Bruce said they had given him my number and was wondering if I might need some repairs.

It just so happened that my bike did need some work. We made arrangements for me to drop the bike off at his house. I explained to Bruce that when it rained sometimes it was difficult for the ignition to work.

In the time you said 'gone' on eBay, he found an ignition switch for me and replaced it. From that point on we developed a very strong relationship. He would work on my bike and I would help him with his computers.

What was different, possibly strange about our relationship, is that we were nothing alike. Our only shared interests were motorcycles. We would go for rides on the weekend. We would always go to Bike Week and Biketoberfest to salivate over the new bikes.

We had brought along another rider to visit the Kawasaki Pavilion earlier in the week who was interested in joining the excitement of Bike Week. On our way home, we got caught in a downpour. The rain became so intense that I was not able to see over my windshield. I pulled off the road where I could get under a bridge, out of the rain.

Bruce and the other rider pulled over about a mile ahead of me and Bruce started to panic because he did not know where I was. We were able to reach each other by telephone, and I assured him I was okay and would start home again once the rain died down.

Each event I would go to I longed to buy a new bike. Bruce loved working on bikes so much he would find older bikes and rebuild them from the frame up. One time he found an old police motorcycle. This was the same model that was used in the TV show, Chips.

Bruce loved this bike. He tore the bike down to the frame and began rebuilding it piece by piece. Each wire, screw, nut and bolt were meticulously returned to the frame. Completing the rebuild, Bruce painted it a metal flake blue.

Bruce and I were proud of his work. He had researched each part and every part on that bike was the original. We enjoyed travelling from town to town showing off his work. There was never a time that we would park our bikes that it was not surrounded by motorcycle enthusiasts.

There were plenty of stories. People reminisced about the days when the bike was on the TV show, the stars and their favorite episodes.

Our modus operandi during Bike Week was to meet in the small town of Bunnell, Florida. We would stop at a diner and have breakfast. After breakfast we would proceed to Daytona, where we would of course go into the Kawasaki pavilion first, where we were regulars.

The Kawasaki manufacturer would have a customer appreciation day during the week and this event was very large and well attended. It was held at the restaurant Hooters and you could indulge yourself in all you could eat hamburgers, chicken wings, hot dogs and cake. Professional stunt motorcyclists would demonstrate their skills in the parking lot.

Biketoberfest is not as heavily attended as Bike Week. The Kawasaki event that week was held at the

Pavilion itself. There were contests and lots of pizza. Bruce and I would never miss going, especially when Kawasaki trivia was being played. Bruce knew everything about Kawasaki.

Kawasaki had several large displays on eighteen wheelers. Each of the trailers had a large Kawasaki mural on the side. Bruce took his antique bike around to the side of one of the trailers, where he asked me take pictures with his bike and himself in front of the mural.

After the pictures were taken, we decided that we had eaten enough and had won enough prizes. It was time to go home. We said our goodbyes and wished everyone well as we headed home. We rode to the exit gate of the Speedway and waited for the light to change so that we could go out into the main road.

As we left the Speedway area, Bruce let me take the lead. As the light changed I turned left and started across the three lanes of the highway and entered the far lane for the direction where we were headed. As I made the left turn, I accelerated. Reaching the next intersection, at approximately a half or three quarters of a mile away where there was a traffic light, I looked back for Bruce and he wasn't there.

I pulled off to the side of the road and waited. Something strange was happening. No cars were coming up to the traffic light. I was unable to go back, of course, so I had to circle the block and come back around. Because of the traffic and traffic pattern changes, it took me a while to return to the spot where I had entered the highway.

Turning onto the Speedway road I noticed the flashing red and blue lights. I was able to take my bike through all the traffic until I reached the emergency vehicles. There was a bike lying on its side. The medics were doing CPR on Bruce. I parked my bike and tried to get through the police barricade. They would not let me through. I tried to explain to them that we had been riding together.

I became numb. I could not get close to Bruce, but I could see his life's fluids running away from his body. His helmet lay flattened. They pulled a stretcher out and I watched as four or five paramedics lifted him onto the stretcher that was now lying beside his body.

They lifted the stretcher to put it into the ambulance. I asked how he was and the paramedic replied with a question, "Was I a family member?" I couldn't lie because he was white, and I was black. I asked if I could ride along. He said I couldn't and told me what hospital they were taking Bruce to.

I felt so totally helpless. I went to the hospital, just a mile away. Parking my bike, I dismounted and found that my knees were weak. Struggling to gain my strength, I entered the emergency area, going to the desk and asking about Bruce's condition.

I was asked if I were family. I should have said yes. That I was a black man and obviously not family, I figured they would catch on to that quickly.

I went to the far side of the emergency ward and searched my telephone for his wife's number. Actually, I was looking for his home number. Panic started to set in again. I did not know his home number, we had always communicated by cell phone.

I did not know his wife's number. There was never a reason to call her. I called a couple of friends who were acquaintances of both of us, to see if they had a home number. None of them did. Somehow in all my panic I remembered that Bruce prepared motorcycles for the motorcycle safety program. They happened to use Kawasaki motorcycles.

Using the browser in my telephone I was able to get the telephone number of the school. I was very lucky to reach them and even better, they had the home telephone number.

I called Bruce's home and his wife answered. I explained to her the best I could what had happened. His wife, Joy, got in her car and drove quickly to Daytona Beach. She was going to meet me at Halifax Hospital.

When we met I took her to the desk where she explained that she was his wife and I was a close friend. We were directed to the elevators and to one of the upper floors.

We were shown to a room where we sat down and I explained what had happened. I explained that I didn't know exactly what his condition was because I wasn't able to get close enough.

They wouldn't share with me any information because I wasn't a family member. It would have been interesting to see their reaction if I had said I was his brother. Being as close as we were I felt we were brothers.

How long we sat there and chatted I don't know. Eventually a woman came in with a man, who I knew was the doctor. The woman could have been a doctor also, but I think she was a nurse. He explained that Bruce had injuries to his head and the force of hitting his head was so great that his brain was severely damaged.

Bruce had died. I can still hear the scream that came out of his wife. She grabbed me and just cried. I became numb again.

It took some time for me to find out exactly how the accident happened. When I turned left onto the divided highway, a motorcyclist behind me decided to go in between us. Because we were so close together he didn't have a lot of room and hit the front tire of Bruce's bike. This caused Bruce to lose control.

What I don't understand is how my friend hurt his head so badly when he was wearing a helmet. Safety was number one for both of us when riding.

Bruce and I were best of friends who had nothing in common. Nothing but motorcycles. We didn't like each other's music or food. We did not hang out together. Bruce didn't drink but we loved to ride.

I stopped riding for a year. I have not been riding very much since. It has been almost four years. I miss Bruce. I haven't found anyone to work on my motorcycle. Sitting in the garage, I know if he were around he would be telling me to get the hell out of the garage and go riding.

If you lose your self-respect, you also lose the respect of others. **Yiddish**

Want Respect, Give Respect

Our family was the first family of color to move into a neighborhood in North Philadelphia, which was predominantly Irish. There were several privately-owned stores on many of the corners and most of these merchants were Jewish. I eventually learned derogatory names for both, which was unacceptable to my mom.

I was old enough to know it was wrong to use derogatory ethnic terms. Children repeat what they hear. My baby sister, Cheryl, had not fully understood the ramifications of name-calling. At least not in front of my parents.

My little sister had to be about seven or eight years old. Mom was in the kitchen, I was reading a *Life* magazine in our living room. Not looking up I heard my little sister say she wanted to go to the store. Mom asked her what store. My sister replied, "to Jew Mary's." That's when the fireworks started. Being funny and cute my little sister was the family favorite. That was all lost with her reply to Mom.

Mom shot out of the kitchen. Grabbing little sis by the arms, she began shaking her violently. I stood there in shock. While Mom was shaking her she shouted, "How would you like to be called nigger, Cheryl? How would you like to be called nigger, Cheryl?" Mom stopped shaking her and sternly explained that there would be no name-calling in our home.

I was just as guilty of using that term. There was no doubt in my mind that my sister had heard me use those words. From that day on I have been cautious about my use of terms for ethnic identity. Lesson learned. My thought was what would she do if I had said that?

Experiences like that were opportunities for growth. I strengthened in tolerance, wisdom and relationship skills. Along the way I gained many lifelong friendships. Can I tell you about Sean?

When you give vent to your feelings, your anger leaves you. **(Unknown)**

Sharing My Culture

Sean's Wife's Birthday Present

Sean was a senior IBM electronic technician at the Rochester lab, who was not only a hard worker but also very knowledgeable in the field of electronics. Without him it would have been difficult at best for me to survive as an electronic technician. Sean became my friend and mentor.

Boom Box

I had an Associate Degree in Industrial Electronics. That was twenty years ago and mainly used for my hobbies. Sean pushed me to expand my limits. We worked side-by-side designing and constructing test equipment for early computer hard drives.

We worked and ate together. Our relationship broadened to social time outside of work and I visited his home several times meeting the members of his family. Sean had three boys and a girl. The youngest son was about five or six years old when I first met him.

During one visit I had my new miniature Schnauzer. This was the first time the youngest boy had met my dog. Being concerned that the dog was not fully housebroken, I held him in my arms. Sean's son was infatuated with the new puppy.

He constantly asked me to put the dog on the floor so he could play with him. It was difficult to explain that the dog might have an accident. Never the one to miss an opportunity, this struck me as a time to have some fun.

I replied, "I can't, the last time I did that he ate the little boy. He was about your size." Sean's son freaked out and ran to tell his mother about this boy-eating dog. A dog that weighed approximately six pounds! Sean and I laughed about this for many, many months.

While constructing test equipment one afternoon, Sean paused for a moment. He asked me if I knew of a gift he could get his wife for her birthday. I replied with the usual ideas, "How about a box of candy, some flowers, or maybe some perfume?"

To each of my suggestions Sean said he had been married long enough to have bought those things many times over. We then returned our focus back to the task at hand.

After some time, Sean shouted out, "I got it!" He had decided on a present for his wife.

Being inquisitive I asked what he going to purchase. Maybe I could use the advice later myself. He went back to work replying, "Never mind it wasn't important."

I shot back, "Hey, we've been discussing this for several hours I have a right to know." I observed that the more I asked the more he tried to avoid me. This was unlike Sean.

Finally, I said, "Sean, you owe me an answer."

He said "Okay. I'm going to get her a nigger box."

I was shocked speechless for a moment. "What?"

Sean repeated it again.

"What the hell is a nigger box?" I asked. I was now on the verge of losing it.

He said, "You know what a nigger box is. Mel, you know what I mean."

I assured Sean that I had no idea of what he was talking about. Then came his reply: "Those large music boxes black guys carry around on their shoulders."

This was the end of the 80's when urban youth carried around huge portable systems. I stated, "What you mean is a boom box." I inquired where had he learned his term for a boom box?

Sean replied, "That's what everybody calls them." I assured Sean that everyone did not choose that term to describe the boom box. I told him, "You are my friend. You mean no harm. For the sake of our friendship, I strongly suggest that you not use that term again. They are boom boxes."

He looked confused and asked, "What's wrong with what I said?" Sean did not seem to know.

Sean knew that the use of that word was not acceptable in conversation or to describe a black person. He thought that using it as a slang term to describe an item was acceptable. After some discussion, Sean began to understand.

I let him know the danger of using it in public in any form. "Sean, if you had said that to any person of color, there would have been a serious problem." After discussing my concerns, Sean began to understand.

You may say that Sean knew that it was wrong. Under different circumstances, I would have agreed with you. This was Rochester, Minnesota, located in the middle of cornfields, and they had a void in their cultural growth. This was a town with a population of 110,000, with only 400 persons of color, including children.

Sean was aware it was wrong to use the term as a description of a person. He thought it would be acceptable to use the 'n' word to describe an item. I am positive he did not know to what depths of anger he could have stirred in the mind of some stranger of color. I could have gone to Human Resources causing all kinds of drama.

Sean and I are still the best of friends. When possible, he visits from Rochester. He stays at my home. We enjoy each other's company. Trust me, I'm sure he's never used that term again. At least not around me.

When we listen to each other we can find common ground.

There is no wise response to a foolish remark.
Slovakian

Hey, My Man

IBM's Rochester lab and manufacturing campus consisted of 5,000 employees. The lab's workforce was a combination of programmers, engineers, machinists, electronic technicians, manufacturing line employees, maintenance workers, custodial personnel and a full line of management and administrators.

This did not include numerous vendors and contractors who supported IBM, such as cafeteria, shipping and waste removal persons and a group charged with the internal moving of office furniture.

The lab was dynamic, exciting and constantly in a state of flux. Projects would start, and projects would end. Walls would be torn down, walls were built up. New equipment replaced the old equipment. That meant that people and furniture moved from one place to another then back again.

IBM professionals were not always congenial with the vendors. This might have derived from the fact that many IBMer's thought they were superior. IBM employees were always knee-deep in their responsibilities.

They were not the best friends or family types. When they went home they would sign on to their computers continuing where they left off at the lab. Understand, this is a very broad generalization. Not everyone was like this.

Several times I witnessed employees acting unprofessional to the custodian and moving staff. The lab employees didn't see them as IBMers. Not being comfortable with that attitude I jumped in when possible to assist in the moving of my furniture and belongings. At times we would sit and chat. I developed several good relationships.

One of the movers and I became quite friendly. He knew I'd stepped in to lend a hand. That seemed to strengthen our relationship. One Friday evening I visited one of the local night clubs. Searching for my friends from CSAL #7 (Concordia School of Adult Learning) over the loud music I heard, "Hey, nigger my brother."

This could not be happening. Was I misinterpreting what I heard because of the loud music? At first, I chose to ignore what I thought I heard. This was not the beginning of a happy evening. I heard it again this time loud and clear.

Turning around to see who the idiot was and focusing on the area where I believed the comments came from, I observed a man and a young lady sitting at a high table. Approaching the table, I asked if he was talking to me.

He replied, "Don't you remember me? I'm the guy you helped move the furniture in your office a couple days ago." Now I recognized him. Acknowledging him I felt quite awkward. His girlfriend caught my eye. His girlfriend was pale as could be. She was slowly sliding under the table.

Returning my glance back to the man on the stool, I pointed out that that was a very unusual greeting. I inquired, "Where did you come up with the idea of greeting me that way?"

His reply was surprising: "When I was in Nam I used to hang out with the black brothers. That's what we used to call each other."

I explained to him that in the service that might have been acceptable. Outside the service black people were uncomfortable with that greeting. We had a good conversation about the unusual situation in which we found ourselves.

He had returned from the jungles of Vietnam back to the cornfields of Minnesota. His time in Vietnam was very special. He had developed exceptionally strong bonds with his army companions. This was his first opportunity to interact in conversation with someone of color since his service days.

I don't accept that most people using the term are ignorant to its meaning. I am saying, why not take the opportunity to find the common ground first. Seek to understand. Try not to be negative. Communication is such a powerful tool. It should be the first remedy for most problems.

Most times misunderstandings could be eliminated in racial situations quickly and easily if both sides would try communicating with each other. Use the opportunity for education for both parties. If one or the other takes the low road, there will be problems.

I had met another soul on common ground.

Better to see the world than not to see it. **African (Fulani)**

Welcome to my World

The friendship between Steve and I grew. Steve included me in his passion to bring minority programmers and engineers to the Rochester lab. Human Resources (HR) teamed us together as recruiters. We were assigned to several colleges.

Tuskegee University of Alabama was one of the campuses we visited. The Tuskegee University staff and students enjoyed our visits. Before we left one recruiting visit, a professor asked if we would assist students with their interviewing skills. HR allowed us to return for a couple of days.

Each student was interviewed on video. After the videoing taping, Steve and I would critique their performance. Steve and I would switch roles from interviewer to cameraman. It was nice to hear that our guidance was well appreciated.

During the day we were invited to have lunch on campus. For me, the campus cafeteria was like eating at Grandma's. This was a new experience for Steve savoring collard greens, real southern fried chicken and sweet potato pie. As we were crossing the campus heading for the cafeteria, I could feel that Steve was uncomfortable. Sitting down to eat Steve shared his concerns.

During his senior year in high school history class, Steve was exposed to WWII and the Holocaust. The next weekend Steve and his buddies had an idea for a funny prank. They took and burned a cross on a Jewish classmate's lawn. A day or two later the police arrived at his house. They took him in handcuffs down to the police station and they had some long, serious discussions.

Steve admitted to what he did and why. Steve and his friends did not understand the implications of their actions to his classmate's family. In the minds of Steve and his buddies it was a joke and meant no harm. The authorities made it very clear that no other similar events would be tolerated. Since that time, he was quite sensitive to ethnic differences.

As we returned to our interview room, Steve turned to me and said, "I have never been treated so well. I have never eaten so well. Yet, I am a nervous wreck being the only white person on this campus."

I looked him in the eye and replied, "Welcome to my world." We laughed. He had a glimpse of what it was like for me living in Rochester, Minnesota.

Run away from an insult, but don't chase after honor. **Yiddish**

Bikers for First Amendment Rights (BFFAR – Crazy Charlie)

Adrenaline is the fireman's drug of choice. I discovered this after I joined Engine Company #2 in Conshohocken, Pennsylvania. That addiction followed me to  Florida. I took up residence in the city of Palm Coast, which is close to Daytona Beach.

Daytona Beach is one of the most famous and major destinations for motorcyclists. It wasn't long before I found other retired and working firemen who also rode motorcycles.

I was recruited by one of the members of the Red Knights motorcycle club. Though riding is the major activity, supporting the community is a close second. The Red Knights members were active or retired firemen and/or EMT's. I tripped all over myself to join.

Our most popular fundraiser is the poker run. In fact, that is the major fundraising activity for most biker events. Not familiar with a poker run?

Here is the skinny on poker runs. The starting point is the first destination. There are four additional stops or destinations. Usually, the route is within 25 miles of the starting point.

At the starting location, each rider pays an entrance fee. Riders then select a card from a pile of scattered playing cards which are face down. The card name and suit are entered on the rider's poker form. This form has a place for the subsequent cards selected at the upcoming stops.

A map of the poker run route is also provided. The route will consist of the location of the other four bars or restaurants. The riders will then proceed to each of the four locations on the map. At each location they select a card from another scattered face down deck of playing cards and that card's name and suit is entered on the rider's form.

The ride ends at the beginning point. The forms are turned over to the judging committee and the rider with the best poker hand wins 50 percent of the entrance pot. Usually there are three or four levels of winners.

Prizes can be, or include, donated items from local businesses that are supporting the fundraiser. Then the party begins! The rest of the event consists of a free BBQ and occasionally live music. Most events have a 50/50 contest and a drawing for donated baskets of goodies. The collected funds are given to local charities.

One of the frequent stops for poker runs was a local drinking establishment called Bikers for First Amendment Rights, in Holly Hill, Florida. Better known as B. F. F. A. R. Those familiar with the bar called it the BFFAR. This establishment was full of characters.

A sitcom could be written about this place. They are typical of the kind of people you would find in a biker bar. These are hard drinking, hard-working, hard riding, blue collar folks. They call themselves rednecks. I call them friends. Not knowing the real definition of the word, I don't think I've earned the right to use the term.

There are about 150 to 200 people that are members of this establishment. Yes, you must be a member to gain entrance. Being a retired fireman, I was eligible to join. I was their only black member when I first joined the BFFAR and, as of today, I believe I was their only member of color.

Remembering my early days of membership, few were willing to acknowledge me when I entered the bar. One or two would greet me with a hello. For the most part, that was the extent of my welcome.

You might find it interesting that I would frequent this establishment. I found the place intriguing. It took me away from my daily stress. I also got to visit with some interesting people. Plus, the beer was cheap.

It wasn't long before I was treated like Norm from the sitcom Cheers. I'd walk in and everyone would greet me with "MEL!" The transformation did not happen overnight. It all stemmed from one incident.

The owner, Crazy Charlie, became very friendly once he was aware I had been a fireman. During the times we both were there, he made it a point to come over and say hello. About two or three months of being a regular he said he had a story to tell. One weekend a black couple visited the bar.

He said he went over to greet them and tell them about club membership. After the membership was offered, the gentleman asked if his other friends could obtain a membership. The owner said that two or three black people were okay. More than that they became niggers.

The gentleman didn't have any more questions. He paid his bill and left. The owner started to laugh. He thought he was quite humorous. I too paid my bill and left.

It wasn't long before our club prepared for, you got it, a poker run. After learning the poker run route and supporting establishments, I noticed that one of them was the BFFAR.

Waiting until I could have some privacy with the club's president, I informed him that I would participate in the ride. However, when we stopped at the BFFAR, I would not enter. He asked me what my concern was. He was furious when he heard the story. He agreed with me.

The president told the club that if one member was not respected, no member would support that establishment. We were a club of 35 plus members. As the only person of color in the organization, I was surprised and honored by their reaction.

Several months later we were preparing for our main event of the year. You guessed it, a poker run. Red Knights members were given fliers and posters to distribute throughout the two adjoining counties, with each member responsible for their appointed areas.

One of the members was assigned the BFFAR. At the BFFAR, as the member was leaving, he was stopped by Crazy Charlie. He inquired why he hadn't seen any of our members at his bar. The member explained it was because of my experience.

Crazy Charlie was humbled and embarrassed. He explained that he had meant no harm. He had not taken my ethnicity or my feelings into consideration. He told our club member that if I returned he would apologize.

After being told of the owner's reaction, the next time I was in the area I stopped in to see him. He was very apologetic and sincerely sorry. Stating it would not happen again, he asked for my forgiveness. I was asked to return. I accepted his apology.

That was the beginning of a real change in my acceptance. I was asked to attend all of their special events. The other members of the BFARR became good acquaintances. It was about that time that I met Willie.

Ignorance is a voluntary misfortune. **English**

Willie

After acceptance by the bar patrons, I became a BFFAR regular. The bar patrons became very friendly. Except for one person who never sat at the bar. I'd notice him at a table by himself. Every so often I'd buy a round of drinks.

Willie and Friend

One evening while returning from the bar with drinks, I headed for a table where some acquaintances of mine sat waiting. On my way back, I passed in front of the loner. Surprisingly he asked if I would buy him a beer. "No problem," I replied, turning to ask the barmaid to take care of him on my tab.

He was a well-known character at the establishment. Even so, I never observed him holding a conversation with any of the other patrons. He sat alone at the table usually in a denim shirt with the sleeves cut off. He sported long gray hair, pulled into a ponytail that hung about 6 inches down his back.

There was always a red bandanna tied around his forehead. He appeared to be in his late 50's or early 60's. On the pocket of his shirt he proudly displayed a patch of the Confederate flag. Until this request for a drink, we had never spoken. I had noticed that he watched me while I was visiting the bar.

The next time we were both there at the same time, he made the same request for a beer. This time he asked me if I would like to join him. I was a little unsure but agreed to share a beer with him. He introduced himself as Willie. It wasn't long before we were acting like old, long time buddies.

We shared our life stories. Willy explained that he had been a truck driver and loved bikes (motorcycles). His lady friend was the bar waitress and that he was there on the days she worked. Each day after work he would take her, on his bike, to their house.

I noticed that he wasn't friendly with any of the other patrons. As Willy explained, he was a good old boy from the back woods of Alabama. He wasn't comfortable in their presence. They had nothing in common. The more I became acquainted with him the more I was curious about his friendship with me. Asking him was out of the question.

As our friendship continued to grow Willy opened up and shared more of his history. He told me stories of his trucking days, about the small town where he grew up. One evening out of the blue he said, "I really like you."

I replied that I didn't understand. Willie explained that I always conducted myself well. I never drank to excess. I was always friendly and cordial with everyone. I never caused any drama. Best of all there was no drama when I left.

Willie and I were sitting together as usual when he said, "I have something to tell you. Being from Alabama, I never met a colored person who I liked. You are the only colored person I've ever talked to or became friendly with. I want you to know that if you ever need anything to let me know."

I thanked him for his kindness.

Willy's next comment was very surprising: "Mel, I have never invited a colored person to my home. But you may come to my home anytime. Stay the night and put your feet under my table. That is an offer I rarely offer to anyone."

What was so different about me? How did I compare to other black folks he had met? What had I done to make him like me? The reply came quick. I respect you, you respect me. Willie developed cancer and went back home to Alabama.

I miss Willie.

To learn to be industrious takes three years; to become lazy takes three days. **Chinese**

Becoming a Blue Blood

My father was strict but fair. That is according to him. No matter what, he was always looking out for me. I was held to the same standards he held for himself.

I became an employee of IBM in August of 1966. Joining IBM was quite an experience. Blue was the color of IBM's logo. If you were in the IBM family, you were considered a 'blue blood'. IBM'ers were so dedicated, it was said that blue blood ran in their veins.

Mel in IBM days

The hiring process was in-depth and intense. After completing a detailed application, the potential employees were tested for particular skills. If the test was passed successfully there was an interview with a middle line manager.

On the condition the interview went well, the next step was a thorough background and security investigation. Not only was a police background check performed, investigators were sent to interview neighbors and past employers.

Within a week or two of my interview I received a call from Harry Wolfhiemer, the office manager. I was asked if I would like to join the IBM team. Giving him an enthusiastic "Yes!" he then asked me something I thought was strange.

"Do you own a suit?" My assumption is that Mr. Wolfhiemer did not realize that it was a must for black men of the church to have and wear suits.

Growing up in the church, Sundays meant you wore your Sunday best. Men did not enter the church without a suit. Nor did women enter without a hat. I assured him that I did have a suit.

I was informed when and where to be for my first day of work. Unknown to me, I would be one of the first minorities hired by IBM. This happened in the middle of the civil rights movement when large and small companies were looking for qualified black applicants.

This was not an easy task. A good portion of the black male population could not pass the security and/or the education requirements. That's another story. My understanding is that before this time IBM did not hire minorities or Jewish people.

The first day I made sure I was early, dressed in my Sunday best. Dad would have been proud of me. I wore a dark blue pinstriped suit, light blue oxford shirt and blue paisley tie. I thought I was cleaner than the board of health.

A secretary directed me to a medium size room where I was introduced to a second new employee. We both sat waiting in our dark suits anticipating what would happen next.

Mr. Wolfhiemer entered the room taking a place behind a lectern. He began his welcome to IBM: "Gentlemen welcome to IBM. You all look very nice this morning. Except for you Mr. Melvin. Here at IBM we wear white shirts. I don't expect to see you in any other color shirt. A white shirt and dark suit is your company uniform. That is if you want to be an employee of this organization." My confidence went from extremely high to through the floor. First lesson of many.

A six-week training class began. About four weeks into training my mother received a call from IBM's calling service. This was a Saturday evening between nine and ten o'clock. I had just turned 20 and was still living at home.

A little bit of luck is better than a ton of gold.
Yiddish

What KKK Rally?

My mother called me at the home of the young lady I was dating. Not a good thing to have your mother call. She told me that IBM had called leaving information about a service call. This had to be a mistake. I explained to my mother that I had not graduated from class.

My father, being the person he was, grabbed the phone saying, "Your employer called and left an assignment for you. Do it! It could be a test." I tried to explain that this was a weekend. I'm sure there was a mistake. His reply was to do the job first and then let them handle the mistake later.

I returned home to change into my dark suit, white shirt and tie. Grabbing my new service case, I proceeded to go to the location I was assigned. I was approximately seven miles from the house when I noticed that the traffic was starting to get heavy and slow down.

Assuming it was an accident I observed a crowd of people growing larger as I proceeded. People were carrying signs and chanting. I was so focused and intent on fulfilling my assignment I never paid any attention to the signs or the chants. My radio was blasting, drowning out the noise of the crowds. The crowd thinned out within a block or two.

Arriving at the address provided to me, I was surprised to find it was a very large trucking company, consisting of many acres. Several trucking companies were located here, which was not too surprising since this was the waterfront area. The entrance fence was closed for the weekend, so I parked my car alongside the gate. Grabbing my service case, I walked to the gate intercom system.

Being dark it was difficult to see. The announcement button was hard to locate. There had to be some type of buzzer or bell to let someone know I was there. The gate, large lot and big trucks gave me an eerie feeling. All of a sudden, a white bright spotlight fell on me. I turned around. The light made it difficult to see anything else but the dark outline of a police cruiser and two policemen.

These were the well respected and feared Philadelphia Highway Patrol. There they stood in tall riding boots and short strap down hats. The two of them staring at me from the shadows was unnerving. If they were trying to intimidate me, it was working. From the shadows, a deep voice asked me what I was doing. I explained who I was and why I was there.

They asked me for some identification from my company. Luckily, I had just received my new identification that week.

Then they inquired what was in the case I was carrying. When I opened the case, it was filled with all types of tools. Would they think I was a burglar? What were the tools for? I explained that they were tools of the trade and new parts needed to complete my job.

The officer was stern but polite. He asked me if I was crazy.

"Crazy?" I responded.

"Yes, crazy. You just drove through the middle of a Ku Klux Klan rally. What were you thinking?"

I replied that if I were thinking I would not have driven into the crowd. I am sure I heard one of them holding back a laugh. They ordered me to complete my assignment quickly. When I finished I was not to return using the same route I had used to get there.

I replied, "That way is the fastest and easiest way to return home."

Again, I was asked if I was crazy. The policeman continued, "You were very lucky to have driven through a Klan rally and not be noticed. There is a big chance you would not be so lucky the next time."

I returned home using an alternate route. No problem.

Later, I learned that my name had accidently been placed on the over-time list which led to my being called.

Surviving the training, I was assigned to a team. The teams met on Monday morning, which is when the last week's expense reports were handed in. It was also a convenient time to share information and discuss any concerns from the previous week. The managers used this time to share any new policies or changes within the organization.

On my first Monday morning meeting, I was excited to meet my new team. I was now part of a team consisting of approximately ten men. At that time no women were hired for diagnosing and repairing of IBM office equipment. We were called Customer Engineers.

Upon entering the room, I noticed everyone was in small groups. Everyone stopped talking for a moment. Then they returned to their group conversations. There I stood alone in the room of all white men. Realizing that I had to do something to break the ice, in a loud voice I asked, "Is this where IBM meets or is this a Klan meeting?" This got their attention.

That would never happen again.

Respect is for one's superiors, kindness is for one's inferiors. **Vietnamese**

I Didn't Raise You That Way

Philadelphia is my birth city, where I cultivated many friendships and memories. My family members were close by. I was familiar with the city's customs and transportation.  Visiting our country's revolutionary historical sites was one of my favorite pastimes.

The company that employed me offered a promotion with a large increase in pay. This was mine if I was willing to move to Minnesota. I jumped at the chance. Little did I know of the discomfort this adventure would provide.

I moved to Rochester, Minnesota in July of 1984. Rochester is a small town in the south east corner of Minnesota. You could say it was built in the middle of cornfields. The city is built around the campus of the famous Mayo clinic. Rochester had a second major employer, IBM. Mayo clinic was by far the larger of the two. Together they employed more than half of Rochester's population.

Moving to a new location can be difficult. You have to find a home, get the lay of the city, learn how to get to your new job, become comfortable with your career responsibilities. There is also the possibility of understanding a new culture. Don't forget the importance of finding friends.

From the first day of work I found the IBM employees to be gregarious. Outside of work things were different. I had nothing to do. There weren't the old home neighborhood bars with which I was familiar.

The first couple of days at work were uneventful. There was the normal process of getting up to speed technically, meeting my new peers and locating the restrooms. The technical side was much more intense than I ever expected. Life consisted of going to work in the morning, then returning each night to an empty home.

Then the winter came. One minute it was the middle of July. The next minute it was October with daily gray skies and snow. I had moved to the Antarctic.

Rochester was characteristic of a mid-American city. It seemed to roll up its sidewalks after seven o'clock.

My daily routine and the lack of companionship started to wear heavily on me. Gray skies, freezing temperatures, strong winds and snow didn't help. Depression took hold. I found solace in a bottle.

Minnesota winters are very cold and very long. My first winter there was full of depression and homesickness. The stress of relocating, job anxiety and the lack of friends led me to falling into a deep depression. At one point I ended up in Mayo's psychiatric department. This was the beginning of my heavy drinking.

I'd leave work, enter the house, turn on the TV and began to drink one glass of wine after another. During the night the deafening sound of strong winds would keep me awake. It sounded like a moaning voice. The moaning and howling touched the depths of my soul.

I would cry most of the night. In the morning I suffered from hangovers and was very tired. It became a vicious circle, each day falling deeper and deeper into the hole of depression.

During these days I grew closer to my mother. She was the only one I felt that understood. There were times that the depression was so deep and so strong I'd call my mother and not be able to say a word.

One time I was so deep in the hole of depression I called Mom. When she answered the phone, I asked her to just talk. Mom never skipped a beat. She began to talk about her day. I finally pulled myself together and would just cry.

Drinking was the only thing that gave me comfort. In Rochester, I had no friends or place to find refuge. Calling my old friends was useless, they had moved on with their lives. They didn't want to listen to me complain. That bottle of wine became my best friend.

Drinking became an addiction. The drinking started to affect my job. Day after day I would show up at work hung over. What made this unusual was that up to this point, I was no more than a light 'social' drinker. I may have had a glass of wine once or twice a week.

Several times at work I would find myself wandering around the lab without any presence of mind, not knowing where I was or how long I had wandered. One time I ended up in a peer's office and sat down.

And just cried. Being homesick and lonely was getting to me. This sadness increased over several months.

One morning after getting up, I found myself going directly to the refrigerator. Reaching in, I grabbed a bottle of wine. By now I was buying wine by the gallon. I poured myself a glass. As I brought the glass to my lips I heard the voice. It was the voice of my grandmother loud and clear.

The voice was clean and sharp as if she were in the room. "Boy, I did not raise you this way." The words cut through me as if they were a sharp knife. I felt that dummy slap. My body felt like it was being poked with a pitchfork.

I froze in my tracks. I waited. The room became perfectly quiet. I looked around, no one was there. It was like I had been transported somewhere else and returned.

Standing next to the sink, I poured the glass of wine down the sink. I went to the refrigerator and took out the gallon of wine. I poured that down the drain. Alcohol never crossed my lips again for close to a year. During the rest of my stay in Rochester I would stop drinking after New Year's Eve. My next drink would not be until my birthday in late March.

Realizing that the loneliness was going to either drive me insane or kill me, I took time to take a good look at myself. It was time for Plan B. I focused on my work. No more drunken evenings. No more wandering around the lab site.

During the next couple of months of going cold turkey from drinking, I heard that Concordia College of St. Paul was starting a nighttime college class in Rochester.

This was a college program for professionals and would be an accelerated course. Students studied as a group throughout the program. Each student completing the course would graduate with an undergraduate degree. This was a strenuous advanced curriculum. The requirements for acceptance were rigid. Essays and three letters of recommendation were part of the requirements. School had never been my friend. I needed a challenge. This was going to be one hell of a challenge. If my past performance was an indicator of my future performance, I was in trouble.

By this time, I had developed several friendships. One being a Filipino double PhD named Gil, who was married to a Jewish girl. They introduced me to their Rabbi. Two of my recommendation letters were one from Gil and another from the Rabbi. The third was from Steve. Steve you met in another story. I was accepted, no problem.

Joining the class, which consisted of a diverse group of nineteen students, was one of the best decisions I have ever made. The people I met have become lifelong friends. It's been thirty years since our graduation, and many of them are still very close friends.

Two in particular are Gloria and her family and Wes and his family. The class supported me continuously throughout the course. There was not a time when I stumbled that someone would grab me, pick me up and push me forward. They were a true group of angels.

I graduated from high school with the average of C-. I graduated from Concordia of St. Paul with a 3.7 average. Gloria and Wes decided they were going to continue their education. I wished them both well.

However, like the true friends that they are they convinced me that I could go further. This was going to be even more difficult. They promised to support me.

With their influence I enrolled in graduate classes. It was stressful and difficult at times. Of course, working a full-time job added to the challenge. Today I can proudly show you my BA from Concordia of St. Paul and my MA from St Mary's of Winona, Wisconsin.

When the family is together, the soul is in place.
Russian

My New Support Family

Family Portrait

Rochester had two main employers, Mayo Clinic and IBM. I was an employee of IBM. IBM had 5,000 employees, with Mayo having at least twice that many. A good two thirds of Mayo's employees were skilled medical or technical employees. I would say that half of the population of Rochester had a minimum of an undergraduate degree.

After moving to Rochester, I developed a drinking problem and a case of depression. The days were short; sunlight was at a premium. The sky stayed gray for 30-plus days at a time. The temperatures would drop to the single digits. Factoring in the wind chill, it could be as low as -45F.

I realized that to stay sane I had to become active. The activities available to me were foreign. Rochester's resident's snow-shoed, cross-country skied or snowmobiled. IBM had an employee paper. Browsing through the pages I found an article on continuing education. One of the available opportunities was from Concordia of St. Paul.

The college would offer classes in Rochester but to do so they needed a minimum of students. I was not a fan of school. To do well I knew I would have to get out of the house and attend classes. Studying would get my mind off my present situation. I decided to give it a try. The acceptance process required several references, in addition to transcripts from my community college.

Acquiring the transcripts was easy. Being new to Rochester my social circle was small, therefore there were limitations to whom I could ask to be a reference.

During my orientation classes for the IBM lab, I met a gentleman by the name of Gil. Gil was from the Philippines. He was married to a Jewish woman. Seeing that I was acting like a lost puppy, they kind of adopted me.

Gil offered to be one of my references. His Rabbi became another reference. My friend Steve became the third reference. All my life I have had these wonderful interactions and relationships with different cultures and ethnic groups. This was another example of how people would take me in and help me out when I was in need.

Gil and I attended classes together during the two weeks of orientation at IBM. I did nothing but complain about Rochester. Gil finally pulled me aside one day, saying, "Mel, if you want to change Rochester, change yourself."

I was furious. I thought Gil was completely out of his mind. We stopped speaking for a day or two. After having time to think about it, I concluded that he was correct. I now understood. Rochester was not going to change. If anything was going to change it had to be me. I had to accept Rochester for what it was.

The class consisted of nineteen to twenty students, so we had met the required quota. We started out together and ended a year and a half of intense academic instruction together. No one dropped out.

It should not be a surprise that I was the only person of color in the class. I was accepted for who I was, not the color of my skin. We had some strange adventures as a group. Many of us are still close and we became like family. You never knew what might happen.

For instance, one day we were at one of our favorite restaurants, Raspberries. This was one of our favorite meeting places, before and after class, or anytime in-between. Sometimes we would 'allow' our spouses or friends to join us.

One night while we were at Raspberries one of our classmates came through the door dressed as a nun, attired in the traditional nun's habit. She walked up to the group and there she stood. She carried a large radio and placing it on top of a table, she pressed the boom box button and Middle Eastern music began to play.

As the music began, she started to take off her habit. Under the habit, she had a Middle Eastern belly dancer's costume. As the music played, she danced while rattling thin disks and beads on her outfit for at least twenty minutes. This was one of the best times we had as a class. As I said, you never knew what might happen.

Another instance was the "You are the Father" prank. I was working on a project with my classmate Jerry. Jerry and I had finished before the others and he decided we should leave early. He wanted to go and have a beer, which we students did after class.

Jerry had a plan. He was our only classmate with a curfew. He wanted to leave early, have a couple of beers, and get home without his wife knowing. Leaving class early, Jerry would be able to visit the girly bar connected to a disco bar, which was another one of our hangouts.

This establishment was designed so one could walk in one door and be in the disco area. On the other side of the disco there was an opening that allowed patrons to access the stripper bar. No one would ever know.

I was game. We drove to the disco bar and Jerry headed straight for the stripper section. I always sat in the back, just in case I had to leave quickly. This was not the place that IBMers wanted to be seen.

Jerry sat right in front of the stage. This is the place where all the guys with dollars put them into the costumes of the ladies. There I was, sitting up front with Jerry, having a beer and nervously watching the show. Jerry began to stuff dollar bills into the ladies' costumes. Suddenly there was a commotion at the entrance.

I turned around and it was one of the women from our class. She stood in front of me and hollered out, "What the hell are you doing here, Mel? You're supposed to be home with me and the kids. Here you are, spending your money on these women."

At this point, Jerry slumped away from his stool. The lady who was dancing stopped and stared at me. I tried to explain that this was not my wife. My classmate never stopped shouting out profanities at me. Now everyone was looking at me.

I slid off my stool, shyly heading for the disco area, at which time my classmate came marching across the bar. Grabbing me by the jacket, she pulled me out of the bar. The class, who witnessed the whole thing, was in tears with laughter. The people in the bar were totally taken off guard. My classmate 'wife' started out her career as one of the first female lineman.

After graduation she went on to become one of the first women executives for AT&T.

A little for you and a little for me – this is friendship. **Indian (Kashmiri)**

The Adventures of Steve and Mel

Eighteen years of anything can become boring. That's how long I worked in the field diagnosing and repairing IBM equipment. I was ready for change. I was easy pickings when my manager suggested I take advantage of an opportunity.

There were openings at a manufacturing lab in Rochester, Minnesota. He explained that there would be a plethora of opportunities there. The excitement of adventure was too much to resist.

Moving to Minnesota turned out to be one of the best and worst events of my life. In Minnesota I learned to be independent and self-reliant. That is where I also matured. The downside was me losing my footing and falling hard. Being blessed, I was able to rebuild myself on a stronger foundation.

The Rochester lab was where IBM's mid-size computer, the AS400, was manufactured. Five thousand were employed at the plant. In this type of environment employment opportunities are dynamic and ever changing. Working in this large facility it felt like you were in a small city.

The workforce was very mobile, and everyone had the opportunity to enhance their skills, take advantage of training or join the management team.

No more than a year after I had arrived at the Rochester lab, my job was eliminated. In those days companies worked hard to keep their employees by offering new positions. They would look for in-house positions/opportunities that were available. If there were none that fit your skill level, they were willing to train you in another skill.

Here I was in a new location and now I lose my job. My skill level in a highly technical manufacturing site was low which meant finding a new position was difficult at best. The jobs offered to me were ground or entry level positions. Being new to the lab I was without a mentor; I felt like I was being pigeonholed. Human Resources and I could not come to an agreement. I found none of the positions acceptable.

It was at this time a savior and friend to me appeared. A manager by the name of Steve had heard about my predicament. Steve was putting a new team together. This team was going to spearhead IBM's new product, high capacity hard drives.

This was 1991 and IBM was introducing the 0663 Corsair. This was the first disk drive with thin film magnet resistive (MR) heads. It had eight 3.5-inch platters and stored 1GB. The capacity of these drives was 5-20 gigabits of information. That was more storage than anyone would ever need. Right. The cost was around three thousand dollars.

Steve asked me to join his team. Due to this position being highly technical, there was one condition. I'd have to bring my "A" game. The position would have me interfacing with trained technicians, engineers, programmers and managers. I held an Associate Degree in Industrial Electronics. Those skills had not been used in over twelve years.

Steve offered me a position as an electronic technician. He was aware that my technical skills were antiquated and not up to the required standards. I was told I could have the position if I was willing to work hard and gained the knowledge needed to perform at a high level. I am always up for a challenge. Hard work, difficult tasks and managing stress are part of my family's DNA.

Within a week I was in my new role as an electronic technician. I grew in knowledge and earned the respect of engineers and programmers. The most important was the friendship that grew between Steve and me.

He is a friend who aids in adversity. **Indian (Tamil)**

A Friendship Grows

Steve saved my career, but more importantly, Steve saved my life. What brought me to Rochester, Minnesota, was the opportunity to learn programming skills. On arrival, I found out that my new position was filled.

My new manager had filled the position with a friend. He had needed an available slot to hire his friend. I was already an employee, so I was allocated to a lower job. I do my best to avoid confrontations when possible. At first, I held it inside. That was the beginning. I began to spiral down, mentally and emotionally.

The bottom fell out six months later when the department was reorganized. Not having engineering or programming skills, Human Resources could not find any department that would accept me. They searched throughout the lab to find a new position for me.

The lab had few positions available at my grade level. Without programming, engineering or technical skills, the only place was the maintenance department. I refused to go to the maintenance department. I had not moved to Minnesota to move backwards.

Lucky for me IBM was bringing on a new product. They were starting a new subsidiary company. The labs primary product was a medium-size business computer, AS/400. IBM now wanted to develop storage devices for personal computers.

The company was starting from the ground up. At that time, it was new technology. A hard drive small enough to fit in a PC was limited to 20 to 40 megabytes of storage at maximum. IBM had designed a new hard file that would store 1 to 2.6 gigabytes. This was an industry breakthrough. Their cost was in the thousands. Today you can buy the drive of 16 GB for under $20.

Steve's new department assignment was to design and build the testers for these hard files. IBM employees are a very loyal and conservative group. Moving to a new company, even though an IBM subsidiary, would be difficult for most engineers or programmers. We were still IBMers, but our company name was now different. Steve had problems finding qualified people for his department.

My training was on small electronic devices. Steve needed someone who could work on large testers. While working with Human Resources to find suitable department members, Steve was made aware of my predicament. He came to me and asked if I would take on the challenge.

The challenge was if he hired me for his new department I would need to work hard to enhance my skills while assisting his engineers and programmers. I jumped at the opportunity. What I did not know was how far I would fall before my feet struck a solid foundation.

For the next three years I was an employee of Steve. When possible, we would go to some of the finest colleges in the country. Our responsibility was to find qualified minority programmers and engineers. We became very good friends outside of work. I joined his softball team. He took me up in his airplane. He had me buy a snowmobile.

Steve gave me the opportunity of a lifetime.

Mistakes will happen. **American**

The Creation of Wedding Phobia

Steve and I had several adventures. The first one I remember was Steve getting married. Steve had invited me to the wedding, but I had decided not to go. My reasoning was obvious: I would be the only person of color. Steve convinced me that with some of the other department members attending that I knew, I would be fine. He also added that there would be many single women.

The day of the wedding I showed up at the church by myself. Looking around the church there was one other person of color. She was a black woman approximately my age. I felt more comfortable thinking that I would have someone to converse with.

After the wedding we all were to gather at the reception venue, which was some distance from the church. Driving there, I found it was a little difficult to find. Finally arriving and parking my car, I grabbed my gift and headed into a large one-story building.

As I was about to enter the building, two very attractive young ladies walked in the door before me. They seemed like they knew where they were going so I followed them. They came to a small card table with tent cards. Each card had a name and table number.

The ladies proceeded to take a card that was facing away from me. Then they walked through the door. I looked for my card, which was facing towards me. I picked up the card and followed them into the reception hall, putting my gift on a large gift table.

There had to be approximately 300 people or more in the room. I proceeded to go to the table number printed on my card. Finding the table, I discovered that all the chairs had been taken. The people were very nice and called over one of the attendants and asked him to find me a chair.

They all moved around giving me room for my chair. We chatted for a while. It was suggested that I go to the open bar to get a drink. I returned to my chair after ordering a rum and coke and got back just in time for the announcement of the bridal party.

We were all given flutes of champagne. The bridal party couples were announced. The first couple to come in had very strange last names. I did not find this unusual because this was a Norwegian and Scandinavian area. I did not know any of Steve's friends.

Four or five more couples were announced. Again, I did not know the names or faces of any bridal party members. Then we were asked to rise and lift our flutes to the newly wedded couple. The announcer's voice became louder, "For the first time I'd like to introduce Mr. and Mrs…"

I had no idea who these people were nor could I pronounce their name. That is when panic set in. When the newlyweds entered the room, I realized I did not know either one of the them. This was not Steve, that was for sure.

After the toast was given I excused myself and went outside of the room. What was I to do? Was I at the wrong place? I went outside and checked the address. It was the correct address. Re-entering the building, I returned to where I entered the room. That's when I noticed that the table had two sets of tent cards.

The tent cards facing away from me were for the door that was in front of them. The tent cards that were facing me were for the doorway behind me. I walked into the doorway behind me and there was Steve with his friends and family.

Steve hollered out, "Where the hell have you been?" I said I had a little trouble finding the place. I told Steve I needed a moment. Going out into the hallway I had a panic attack. Yes, I had found the correct wedding party. Now my gift was in the wrong room.

What was I to do? I paced back and forth trying to find a solution to my situation. I noticed a man walking down the hallway. He had been the announcer for the bridal party. Approaching him I shared my dilemma. I explained that I had gone to the wrong reception. As a result, my gift was on the table of the wrong wedding party.

He suggested that I go in and pick up the gift and leave. I asked him if he was crazy. There was over 300 white people in that room. You expect me, one black man, to walk in, pick up a present and walk out? At that point I think he understood my situation.

He suggested that he'd walk in with me to get the package. We walked in together, I found my gift, and as I walked out everyone was staring.

Returning to the correct reception, Steve grabbed the gift. He put it up on the table and again asked what took me so long? I explained the whole situation. Steve began to laugh so hard I thought we might have to call for emergency services.

Before I knew it, I was laughing just as hard. After we finally stopped laughing, I inquired where to find the restrooms. Leaving the reception again, I entered the restroom and found the stall. My stomach was killing me. Sitting there the door swung open.

I heard clicking sounds on the restroom floor. Were they high heels? The person took the stall next to me. Looking at the shoes I knew I was in the wrong place.

It was quiet for a while. Then a voice from the next stall said, "One of us is in the wrong restroom."

I agreed, confessing it was me.

The female voice said, "Do you want me to leave first or would you like to leave first?"

I said please would you leave first. She agreed and left after washing her hands.

This was my opportunity to escape. Jumping up I washed my hands quickly and headed for the door.

When I opened the door imagine my surprise seeing that people had lined up on both sides of the doorway. They applauded as I came out of the ladies restroom. Steve stood at the end in tears.

Later when the laughter died down Steve pulled me aside and said, "That was my cousin. She came and let me know that you were in the ladies restroom. I made an announcement to the guests to join me outside the door of the ladies room."

The only thing worse was sharing the information with my mother the following day. I thought that I would get some sympathy from her. It took her weeks to stop laughing.

Steve and I had many laughs about that day.

Danger and delight grow on one stalk. **English**

Snowmobile X Games

One day it was summer and the next day it was winter. Winter in Minnesota was like living in the freezer for six months. You could look outside and see the clear blue sky. The sun would be shining. It resembled looking at a super high definition TV. Stepping out to get the mail your skin would instantly tighten up on your face. Breathing would burn your nose and bring tears to your eyes.

Each day brought another survival lesson. Not all were harsh, though each lesson provided you with tools that would help you survive. Every auto had its own personal emergency kit in the car. Some of the things carried would be a bag of kitty litter, a shovel, a candle, flashlight, several blankets, and at that time a CB radio if possible.

In addition, I added other items including several Hershey bars, more candles, a space blanket, a can of tuna fish, several flares, and matches. All of those items could save my life if I were to be stranded in my car during a Minnesota storm.

Chocolate candy bars could keep your energy up for several days. Candles burning in the car could be the difference between living or freezing to death. The flares and CB radio could summon help.

With winter came loneliness. You had to plan how to stay busy in the winter. Though it was cold outside, life was easier if you found a winter sport to enjoy. Being outside was quite invigorating.

I learned cross-country skiing and when possible, I would take short walks in the woods. Winter in the Minnesota wooded area must be the quietest place in the world. It is so quiet it could be haunting.

Steve decided he would not only be my boss, he also took on the mission of helping me develop a social life. Rochester was a town of 110,000 of which 400 were of color. That 400 included men, women and children. Steve and I met on a college recruiting trip. Steve was easy to converse with; therefore I was able to share with him the concerns of the young black programmers and engineers that we were trying to recruit.

We recruited at colleges such as Penn State, University of Texas at Brownsville, Tuskegee University, NYC College of Technology and the University of Minnesota.

Steve became my social life coach. Steve was a licensed pilot, an electrical engineer and a father of two boys. Our friendship grew after recruiting at the various colleges. As our friendship grew, the adventures began. Our first adventure, I remember, was when he convinced me to buy a snowmobile.

Steve was always concerned that I had something to do. One winter he decided I needed to learn to snowmobile. A friend had a used snowmobile he was selling. Buying it, I waited for the snow. When the first October snow came Steve took me out for several tryouts or shakedown rides.

One night, after a large snow fall, I received a call from Steve to put the snowmobile in the truck and come over to his place. When I arrived at his home there were about ten other people with their snowmobiles. They were going for their first ride across the country side. They positioned me at the end of the line because I was so new. Without any instructions they headed off.

Off we went into the woods.

We went up and down small hills, in and out of trees. Then we rode into a forested area where the path was quite narrow, and we had to stay in single file through the trees. About twenty minutes later we came to a halt.

Our first run of the season came to a stop when the leader hit a dead end. We could not get the snowmobiles through the thick woods.

It seems we could go no further on that path. We had to turn our snowmobiles around. There is no reverse on a snowmobile, therefore each of us had to physically turn the vehicles around. This was achieved by lifting the front end and pulling it around.

These things are heavy, with some of the older riders needing help to lift the machine. It took some time for everyone to get ready to go. Being the newbie, I was the last in line. Turning around was easy for me since I had not entered the woods. All I had to do was turn around. Now I became the leader. What does it say in the Bible about the first shall become last and the last shall become first?

I was now at the front of the pack. Being my first 'real' time on a snowmobile I wanted to see what it could do. I had an open field of snow in front of me, so I gave the snowmobile all the gas it could take. Flying across the farmer's field was so exhilarating, like riding my motorcycle. I must say it was a lot bumpier.

The feel of the wind got my heart pumping. I began to breathe very heavily and my breath on my helmet face shield started to fog it up. Additionally, the snow started to fall again and melted on my windshield. I didn't care. I was flying.

I gave the machine full throttle. This was an opportunity to open this thing up. I flew across the white snow. Due to the speed of the snowmobile and the snow melting on my face shield, I was not able to see very far. Did I slow down?

Hell no. There was that moment of clarity when I realized I could not see. The snowmobile went flying across an open field. The motor started a high whining pitch. That was when I realized I had a problem.

Something told me to look down. I was no longer on snow. I couldn't see anything below me. I had gone off an embankment. Terror set in. That's when I heard the scream of a savage.

It took me a second or two to realize it was me. The snowmobile fell flat on the bottom of the crevice and the drop pushed the seat of the snowmobile into my crotch. I was sitting on my testicles.

The boys were hanging out to party. There is no way I can describe the pain. The pain was so great my toenails curled back and I never let go of the throttle. Now the snowmobile had traction. It flew across the bottom gaining speed. Approaching the opposite side, the snowmobile started climbing up.

I'm told I looked like the launch of the space shuttle. In the air I did a beautiful 180-degree turn going straight up. NASA astronauts would have been in awe.

The snowmobile came crashing down on the edge of the embankment. I was lying on my side with the snowmobile on top of me. The other riders had caught up with me. Over the laughter I heard Steve say, "If you want to learn to jump, I'll teach you that the next time we go out."

I sold the snowmobile.

The more danger, the more honor. **English**

"Want to see a pencil float?"

Steve was my manager and a close friend. It was quitting time early one spring day when Steve barged into my office. He was restless and decided that he would take me flying.

A Flying VW

Steve was a licensed pilot who had hundreds of hours of flying time. In his spare time Steve was building his own plane from a kit which was called a Canard. The wings swept forward as opposed to the rear. The project took up all the space in his garage.

Steve decided that this was a not only a good time to fly, it was a great time to take me along on my virgin flight. I became very creative in avoiding this adventure. This time I was caught off guard and

Steve was determined. Steve had decided that I should be a pilot.

We drove down to the airport. Rochester had a small, international commercial airport which was crucial in getting patients and doctors to and from Minneapolis, especially in the winter. It was not unusual for private planes the size of commercial planes to use its landing strips.

Leaders from the Middle East, presidents and celebrities were known to use the services and facilities of the Mayo Clinic. Some of the celebrity patients that visited Mayo Clinic while I was there included Muhammad Ali, the King of Jordan and President Ronald Reagan as well as many well-known TV and movie celebrities.

When the King of Jordan came he had two full-size commercial planes. He traveled with his family and security personnel. Rochester was transformed with his visit. It was amazing to see and experience what real money could do. The king and his large entourage, which included escorts for the women, took over the city. The wife or any other woman could not be in a room alone with male doctors.

Arriving at the airport Steve and I proceeded to a small building where he rented an airplane. After the flight documents were completed, we were off to a plane sitting on the runway. The plane was a Piper

150. You've seen this plane many times, it's very popular.

The wings sit on top of the airplane. It has one small wheel up front and two wheels in the back. Steve began to do a ground inspection of the plane. He was very precise and particular in everything he did. After checking the outside of the plane, we climbed into the cockpit and secured our seat belts.

Now he really had my attention. This was like sitting in an early Volkswagen bug with wings strapped on the top. The main difference was that the vehicle had no backseat and the engine was in the front.

Steve went through a cabin check. Starting the engine, he picked up the radio mic and announced his intentions for takeoff. Steve positioned the plane on the runway and then he was given the OK for takeoff.

The motor came to life as the throttle was advanced. The plane started to move down the runway, began rolling faster and started to lift. As the ground begin to fold away my body was tensed with anticipation. Steve took the plane up in a gentle climb.

Reaching flying altitude, we began to fly over the outskirts of Rochester. Steve began our bird's eye view tour of the town. Flying around Rochester was exciting. Steve showed me his house from the air, which lay on the outskirts of Rochester.

Flying past his home he tilted the plane to the right so that I had a better view from my right window. Flying stopped being fun. I thought I would fall out. I was now looking straight down on the surface of the earth.

How long we flew around like this I don't remember. All I can say is I believe that Steve became a little bored with just buzzing around Rochester. At this point he turned to me and asked, "Have you ever seen a pencil float?"

"A pencil float?" I replied.

"Yes, let me show you."

With that Steve pulled a pencil from his pocket protector. Every IBMer had a pocket protector. Steve placed the pencil on what I will call the plane's dashboard. Then he pulled back on the yoke and began to climb.

Steve gave the plane more throttle as he climbed as high as he could. The plane began to sputter. Hearing the plane starting to die, I became quite concerned. It wasn't from the gravity of the situation. It was the gravity that was trying to pull me through the bottom of the plane.

I held tightly onto the bottom of my seat. Just when I thought the engine would totally cut off, Steve took and pushed that yoke in as hard as he could. At that point the plane went into a steep dive. Fear shut off any vocal response I had. I threw my hands up and I was now pushing on the top of the plane.

My thought was I was going to be pushed out the top. The plane was going down quickly as the motor raced uncomfortably loud. Steve had become uncommonly quiet.

I looked to my left. Steve was knocked out. Yes, Steve was knocked out with his head hanging forward. I swear he was floating!

The plane kept going straight down. On the dash was a red flashing light. It seemed to be saying, you gonna die, you gonna die, you gonna die!

I had no idea of what to do. The plane slowly began to come out of the dive. Did I say slowly, very slowly? Before I knew it the plane was flying level. Steve woke up shaking his head.

He asked me what had happened.

I was shouting, "What happened? What happened? How the hell do I know?" Steve took control of the plane and took us back to the airport. As the plane touched the ground I could feel my innards starting to relax.

Returning to the same spot we had found the plane, Steve and I looked at each other with a quizzical look on our faces. As the plane came to a stop, Steve yelled out, "I know what happened!"

I was baffled as to why he was so happy. "What are you talking about?"

Steve replied, "I know why I was knocked out."

"Why?" I asked.

He screamed that his seat belt was unlocked.

I looked over and observed his seat belt was hanging loose. Not until he tried to release it did he realize it was undone.

He diagnosed that when I threw my hands in the air, my hand had unbuckled his seat belt. This allowed him to hit his head on the top of plane knocking himself out when he put the plane into a dive.

I asked him why the plane started to level out on its own. He replied that this was a plane used for training. It was designed to fly level if the yoke was left free; the trim was set to automatically return the plane to level flight.

We broke out in laughter. The laughter came hard and steady. We stumbled out of the plane as though we were drunk, finding it difficult to stand up from the pain of laughing.

Another adventure with Steve was over.

There were many lessons to learn in Rochester like developing new friendships, learning a different value system, learning to laugh at myself.

My friends have no bounds when it came to playing a practical joke on me. You never knew when it was coming. What follows are a couple of examples of their creativity…

It is better to be alone than to have a bad companion. **Philippine**

The Legend of the Inflatable Doll

For three and a half years I buckled down and focused on getting an education. The first year and a half I worked on my undergraduate degree. I had an Associate Degree when I moved to Minnesota. Attending classes after work was not easy but was worth the effort.

When I started going to classes back in Philadelphia many of my peers questioned why I was attending college classes. IBMers were aware that if they did a good job, they would be taken care of until their death. IBM had an extensive training program. Being an international company, there were few professions or trades that you could not find available in the company.

What a surprise when the department I was with in Rochester decided to give me a luncheon. They seemed to be generally proud of me. Honestly, I was proud of myself.

I have a learning disability called dyslexia. It held me back all through high school. In fact, it was one of the contentions between my sisters and myself. They did very well in school while I struggled. To attend college classes, I had to develop my own way of studying.

The day of the luncheon Steve, my manager, invited his manager to join us. We went to one of the local restaurants where the department bought me lunch. After lunch they decided to honor me with gifts to show their appreciation of my accomplishments.

Anyone outside of my department would have thought that this was a bachelor's party. The items that I was given were quite embarrassing. The second line manager, who was Steve's boss, seemed to be a little uncomfortable as the gifts were opened and passed around.

Finally, there was one last gift. One of the guys got up and shared that he realized that finding black women in Rochester was difficult. Therefore, the department had chipped in to help me out.

When I unwrapped the box, I found a black inflatable doll. This was the ugliest thing I had ever seen in my life. The department broke up in laughter. It became worse as they passed it around the table.

When it got to the second line manager, he was so conservative and concerned about his position, he almost threw it at the next person as it came to him. I gathered my gifts and thanked them all for their kindness. Then I placed the items in my car to take home.

Of course, my friends from my college classes found out about the inflatable doll. One night while we were having dinner at a local restaurant, I heard an announcement over the PA system.

"There is a brown Toyota in the parking lot. The lights are not on but there is an inflatable doll in the back seat and her vibrator is on."

I panicked. How did they get that doll? There was no way they could have gotten their hands on that doll. It was a class prank. It did not lessen the embarrassment.

I had taken the doll and thrown it in one of the closets. Even though I had forgotten about it, I had also forgotten that I had shared that information with my classmates. They found this hilarious.

No, that's not the end of the story of the inflatable doll. The winters in Rochester were long. I'm going to use the excuse that I was bored and was looking for something to entertain me and came across the doll.

It had never been taken out of its packaging. I thought it was so ugly that I had no idea why anyone would buy the thing. Being the curious person, I decided to inflate it to see what it really looked like.

After inflating the doll fully, it was even more unpleasant. What's more, it had holes in places mama had not told me about. I wanted to get rid of this thing immediately. I attempted to deflate it.

I could not figure out how to get the air out as there seemed to be some type of locking system to hold the air in the doll. Not knowing what else to do, I took the doll, fully inflated, and just stuffed it back into the closet.

Years later I had the opportunity to move to Florida. In packing my things and cleaning out closets, I ran across the inflatable doll. It was still fully inflated. I was determined now to deflate this doll, even if I had to stick a pin in it. For some reason I was now able to figure out how to let the air out. After deflating the doll, I placed it back in the closet to be disposed of later.

When I was preparing to move, several of my friends offered to help me pack. One of them was Margie, with whom I had become very good friends. Margie offered to help me clean out the closets and pack boxes.

When I came across the deflated doll, I prepared to throw it into a plastic bag and get rid of it. Margie, seeing it, demanded that I give it to her. I asked her why. She said that she wanted to show it to her partner. I was glad to get rid of it. I trusted her to get rid of it.

My friends decided to throw a going away party for me. I had volunteered at many of the nonprofits in the city, therefore many of their officials also came to the party.

I was the chair of the human rights commission for both the city and the county and there were several persons from that organization who attended. Many of the friends I had made from Mayo Clinic and IBM joined us. There were people from all over the city that I knew, and those I did not know, who attended the party.

The party was held in a nightclub. The idea was to party where no one had to clean up. My friends came bearing going away gifts for me. I received everything from boxer shorts to model tractors. Most of the gifts were gag gifts. There was one large box that I was instructed to open last.

It was so exciting to get such a large box. The box was approximately three feet high and two feet wide. I was instructed to unwrap it, then I was to grab one of the box flaps and give it a good pull.

How could I have been so gullible? After all this time in Rochester I should know these people. I yanked the flap hard. I heard a snap, then a hissing noise. Then it happened. A rubber leg flew out of the box. I did my best to stuff it back in the box, but I was pulled away.

Then a second leg popped out of the box. Before you knew it, a fully inflated doll was now emerging from the box. Margie, my bosom buddy, had taken the doll and given it to the engineers in my department.

My programming and engineering buddies had connected an air cylinder to the doll. Then they placed them both in the box and sealed it. By pulling the flap I released the air into the doll.

To this day when I return to Rochester there is someone who talks about the legend of the inflatable doll. Trust me, no one will ever see that doll again. I made it an offer it couldn't refuse.

A trick is clever only once. **Yiddish**

Steve's Phantom Breakfast

The pressures of the job began to take its toll. We were coming closer to the deadlines to bring the project online on time. Each of us was putting in as much time as possible. Steve started to come to work earlier in the morning to get as much of a head start as he could.

During one of our department meetings, Steve mentioned that he was getting to work early. So early in fact that he couldn't have breakfast. In our department we had an engineer who was quite proficient in pranking.

The engineer decided to get in earlier then Steve, this way he was able to place breakfast on Steve's desk. When Steve arrived, he found the breakfast on his desk. He began to question each of the team to find out which one had left the breakfast.

Nobody would admit to it. The next morning the same thing happened. Again, Steve inquired who had bought him breakfast.

This went on for months. Steve did everything he could to figure out who was buying him breakfast. I don't remember how it started, but we began to switch off on who was going to buy breakfast for Steve. This made it even more difficult for Steve to solve the breakfast mystery. Steve never could figure out where his phantom breakfast came from.

Humor is like a cosset lamp. **American**

A Moment of Karma

I was guilty of several practical jokes. The two I am most proud of was when a new telephone system was installed. This was a state of the art system with all the bells and whistles. For the 1990's this was the Swiss Army Knife of telephone systems.

It could do just about everything. It recorded calls, could call several people at one time for a conference call, it had an intercom. But wait, there's more. The regular intercom provided a tone on the receiver to let the person know they were being paged. You could leave your message or speak directly to the receiving person.

I was writing a testing robot instruction manual. It was a very boring, slow day. Needing some information, I proceeded to call one of the engineers. Forgetting how to use the intercom I located the instruction manual to find the procedure.

But by chance I came across a procedure that would let me leave a message without the tone. This would let you start speaking with no tone. So, I decided to try it out. I dialed Steve's number. When it let me know I was connected, I said into the receiver, "Steve this is God. Are you working?" Then I hung up.

No more than about two or three minutes later, I can hear Steve going up and down the hall sticking his head into each office. I could hear him inquiring who had made the call.

Of course, no one knew what he was talking about. Finally, he came to my office and asked, "Had I called?"

I said, "No, It wasn't me. What are you talking about?"

He then said, "Are you sure it wasn't you?"

I assured him it was not me.

Steve said the phone started talking by itself.

"What did the voice say?"

"It said this is God and asked me if I was working."

It took everything I had not to lose it at that point. Again, I assured him it was not me and he left.

I never told him I was the culprit playing God on his phone. It was karma.

Then there was Secretary's Day. Steve was going to take his secretary to lunch. We were all asked to join him, as Steve did not want to have lunch with his secretary by himself. Everyone agreed to go. When Steve left for a meeting, I did the rounds again. This time I asked everyone to make up an excuse why they couldn't go.

Steve got back to his office just before lunch. That's when his phone began to ring and each of us explained why we couldn't attend lunch. Steve became a nervous wreck. You should've seen the relief on his face when we all showed up at the restaurant.

Karma strikes again.

It is the safest sailing within reach of the shore.
Dutch

Captain Mel

There is no way to express how excited I felt when I discovered sailing classes in Rochester. Educational opportunities for adults was an important part of the community. There were adult classes available and at very affordable prices.

Rubber Ducky

So off I went to learn to sail. Having to learn knots, the different sails and their sail positions was not what I expected. I was ready to go on board a boat and start to sail. What I learned most importantly was the fact that safety was the most vital lesson in sailing. A silly mistake could be disastrous.

The classes lasted approximately four weeks, learning nautical nomenclature and how to read the weather. Most importantly we learned boating safety.

After passing a written test and a test to show your ability to tie certain knots, we were asked to meet at the community pool.

Here each of us had to go through a swimming test. Once we passed our testing, we could show up at Lake Pepin which was part of the Mississippi River. There we had the opportunity to learn to sail on a boat called a Sunfish.

The easiest way for me to describe a Sunfish is to say it is a very large surf board with one triangular sail. We were taken out one at a time, with actual sailing classes starting on May 30. What we students did not know is that in Minnesota the water never gets warm.

I noticed that my instructor had a wet suit on. He pushed the Sunfish into the lake while I got on board and then we sailed out approximately 100 yards or so.

At this point he explained he was going to tip the boat over. Once the boat was tipped over he demonstrated how I was to right the boat again. Well, the boat and I went into the water.

I might as well have jumped into a glass of ice water. What an awakening. Righting the craft was not the first thing on my mind. I was freezing. Then desperation sits in. You want out of the water.

So, you work very diligently to right that craft. This would happen three times before you were qualified to sail on your own. I was losing the thrill of sailing quickly.

The sailboats were available to every student who had passed all the tests. Each week I would go and practice. When you feel comfortable there is one more test. After the final test you could sail on your own.

Securing my sailing certificate, I was very proud of myself for passing all the tests. I was happy to take anyone out who was willing to sail with me. One summer Samantha, my daughter, came to visit. She, my friend Kathy and I were on the Sunfish sailing on Lake Pepin.

Son of a son and his daughter Samantha

It was getting to be the middle of the summer and the breezes on the lake we're not as strong as usual. Samantha became bored that we were moving along so slowly. She wanted to go faster.

Kathy was holding onto the main sail line. If you are not familiar with sailing, the main sail acts as an accelerator. When you pull the sail closer to the boat, the faster the boat goes and the more it heels over.

The idea is to have the boat move as quickly as possible.

I asked Kathy to bring the sail in a little bit and the boat began to gain speed. The boat heeled over just a bit and Sam started to enjoy the ride again. The breeze would come and go.

As a result, the Sunfish would pick up a little speed, didn't slow down, and would pick up speed again. One thing that was important to look out for is gusts of wind. After some experience you can pretty much predict when it was going to gust.

Having two people on board, I could not let my attention lapse. I felt the breeze begin to strengthen. I called down to Kathy to let out the sail. She let it out some, but the wind kept gaining strength.

I hollered to Kathy to let it out. Finally, it was so strong I instructed her to just let it go. Too late. The Sunfish flopped over with a big splash. The three of us were thrown into the water. Knowing all the safety rules, each of us had on a life vest.

Samantha was approximately six or seven years old at the time. The excitement of being thrown in the water was a little more than what she had expected. When we were all back on the boat, Samantha, with a stern look, pointed and shook her finger and said to Kathy, "When daddy says let go, let go!"

Kathy and I could not stop laughing. This little girl had her fill of excitement that afternoon. This is one of my many fun memories of sharing with my daughter.

One of my peers at work, Griffey, asked if I would take him sailing. We left work early and off we went to Lake Pepin. He brought along a cooler containing six cans of beer. Of course, my passenger wanted some excitement of the boat heeling over. Remember Samantha?

Drinking beer and not paying attention to the wind, we were in an open area when a gust came and blew the Sunfish over. We were both thrown into the water, along with the beer cooler. Not a problem.

While we were in the water, I righted the craft and Griffey climbed aboard. At that point the Sunfish began to slowly move forward. I swam to catch up with the boat.

Griffey noticed that the beer cooler was floating away from the boat. He abandoned the boat, jumping into the water to rescue the beer. With no one in the boat, it began to sail faster. Now both Griffey and I were in the water and the Sunfish sailed away by itself.

I had to put energy into my swim to catch up with the boat. Luckily one of the lines was dragging from the rear of the boat and I was able to swim fast enough to get hold of it. How would you explain it if you lost your Sunfish while saving a six pack of beer?

Sailors are a tight knit group of men and women. Learning to sail I formed a friendship with one of the instructors. As my sailing experience and skills increased, I was asked to become an instructor. After instructing for a year, several of the instructors shared with me that they would return boats from Mackinac Island back to Chicago. They asked me if I was interested in doing this.

The way this worked was a boat owner from Chicago would enter a race, which took place from Chicago to Mackinac Island. This was approximately a four to eight-day race. People from around the world would come to compete. Crews would practice on weekends and take their vacation time to prepare for the race.

The responsibility of my instructor friends was to drive up to Mackinac Island and sail the boat back to Chicago. This way the original crew used less of their vacation days. The racing crew would drive our vehicle back to Chicago. When we arrived back at Chicago we would then get another vehicle and drive home.

The first time was very exciting for me. A racing boat is much different from a pleasure craft. Comforts are sparse. Everything is made for speed. The beds were hammocks that dropped from the ceiling. Once you were in the hammock you used pulleys that would roll you into a cocoon toward the inside of the boat.

This way, if the ship shifted, you would not fall out. Cool, safe but not comfortable. There was no place to sit or lay that was comfortable. There were always two or three pieces of equipment poking at some part of your body.

The first night we slept on board was interesting. There had to be hundreds of sailing boats. So many that they could not all dock at the harbor. So, the method was to dock each boat, tying them side by side. This meant to get to the dock you had to cross over six, seven or eight boats. That becomes more exciting when you must go to the bathroom in the middle of the night. Sailors sleep anywhere they can, especially after a race and they have partied all night.

The next morning, we started our trek home down the western side of Michigan. The first night we were unable to find a place to dock. So, we anchored out on Lake Michigan.

When we arrived at the next dock it was full. Again, we tied up next to another boat. We were about four boats from the dock and it wasn't too uncomfortable climbing over the sides of the boats to get to the dock. Once getting to the dock you could use the facilities of the harbor.

If you've been camping then you are familiar with the communal showers, bathrooms and washing basins. I followed my fellow instructors over four or five boats on to the dock and then to the facilities. There must've been about 15 to 20 wash basins along the wall on the left. On the right there were about 20 showers with an area for getting dressed.

When we entered the room, it was full. When I walked in you could hear the showers going and the water running in the basins. Everyone was shaving, showering and brushing their teeth. And then they noticed me walking through the door. The place went silent except for the water running.

Those who were in the showers stuck their heads out because they knew something had happened. They all turned and stared at me. You see, I was one of the first blacks who used those facilities.

As quickly as it started everything went back to normal. Except for me. It had not dawned on me how uncomfortable I had made things. I never had a more difficult moment trying to retain my confidence and self-esteem.

We stopped to visit four to five harbors as we continued our journey. Each one of the small towns were like small villages. Venturing out in the evening to walk in the downtown districts, we experienced the pleasure of discovery. We would divide up and go our different ways, each looking for the perfect place to have dinner.

At one time in our trip we had been on the water for several days. We had instant oatmeal every morning and I was looking forward to having a great dinner that evening. I mentioned it to the crew and everybody agreed we were going to have a light lunch that day so we could have a great dinner that evening.

Arriving at the town we all decided to have steak that night at the local steak restaurant. The restaurant lined up several tables so that we could all sit together. I did not drink at the time but one of the crew ordered an old-fashioned alcoholic beverage.

As we sat there waiting for dinner, he had a second old fashion. The next thing I knew he's laid out on the floor. We all ran to and fro trying to figure out what was wrong. It just so happened that one of the crew members was a doctor. Actually, he was a professor.

Rushing to our fallen crew mate's side we helped him up and sat him back in his chair. He began to shake it off. Well, it wasn't too long and he toppled out of his chair again. Someone from one of the other tables ran over and started to do CPR.

The doctor finally pushed this person away and said, "Wait a minute he's breathing and has a heartbeat."

Emergency services were called and they put him on a stretcher and off to the hospital he went. This ended any desire for a steak dinner that night.

We all returned to the boat and waited for results. It was a solemn evening. Each of us sat around moping, wondering how our friend was doing. Several hours later he returned with Mike, the captain. They could not find anything wrong physically.

The diagnosis was that having been out on the water all day, he had become dehydrated and his blood sugar was off. By having the two drinks, the contents were shot into his system and caused him to lose consciousness. On the way home, we were happy for John. However, we all started to mumble and grumble because we had missed our steak dinner.

Well, John did not disappoint us on our next trip the following year. One morning, when we were raising the sails for the first time, John was helping unfurl the main sail from the boom. As it was pulled to the top of the mast, suddenly we heard John yell.

We rushed to see what was wrong. Unknown to John a bat was wrapped in the main sail. Unfurling the main sail John had inadvertently grabbed the bat. To protect itself, it had bitten him. One of the crew, thinking fast, ran and got a box and enclosed the bat in the box. We were concerned that the bat might have had rabies.

Off to the hospital John and Captain Mike go. The rest of us stayed with the boat. At the hospital the situation was explained and eventually they were directed into one of the examining rooms. The doctor came in and asked what the problem was.

Mike explained what had happened. The doctor then asked to see the bite. During the examination Mike explained that they had captured the bat, being concerned it could have rabies. The doctor thought that was a great thing to do and asked where the bat was. Captain Mike said, "Here, in this box," and as soon as he opened the box, the bat flew out.

The doctor freaked out and went screaming out of the examining room and the bat took to the air. It was now flying around the large area. The nurses and patients were screaming, scattering in every direction. After the bat was captured things settled down and both John and Captain Mike were thrown out of the hospital.

Respect others if you want to be respected.
Philippine

RENT-A-COP

There is one incident that stands out very clearly from my sailing adventures on Lake Michigan. That was the day I had one of my most embarrassing encounters.

At one time, we were asked to sail from Chicago to Mackinac Island. This was an unusual sailing request, as this was just the opposite of what we normally would do. Each summer around the Fourth of July we would drive a car to Mackinac Island. There we would pick up the racing boat and sail back to Chicago. Our car would be driven back by the crew that raced the boat to Mackinac Island.

This time the owner of the racing boat had decided to spend some time on Lake Michigan with his family. Therefore, we were going to sail his personal boat to Mackinac Island from Chicago. His family would drive our car from Chicago to Mackinac Island, where we were to switch vehicles. Then he would bring the family back in his personal vessel.

His boat was docked at the Chicago yacht club. This was Chicago's most exclusive yacht club. We arrived and parked our car and proceeded to the craft. We settled in, stowing our equipment away and had some dinner. We needed to get up early the next morning as it would be a long day, so wanted to go to bed at a decent hour.

A couple of the guys decided they were going to go use the rest room of the yacht club before turning in. They left the boat and started down the path to the yacht club.

At first, I had decided not to go to the rest room. As they got halfway there, I realized I might not want to get up in the middle of the night to use the facilities. I decided to catch up with them.

As they were about thirty yards in front of me, I could not hear what was being said to a large black woman, in a uniform who had approached them. They exchanged words for a while and I noticed her acting as though she was sorry by the way her body language appeared.

As I approached her she began to apologize. She kept saying, "I didn't mean anything about it, don't worry about it no problem." It was very annoying because I had no idea what she was talking about, but she kept apologizing. In fact, she then assured me that it was OK that I go into the facilities.

Upon entering the rest room, I noticed that my friends were very quiet. Now I was filled with curiosity. I questioned them about what was going on. Each one assured me that there was nothing going on. That everything was OK.

I asked why the guard was so apologetic. They looked at each other and still said nothing. I became quite inquisitive at this point. Finally, one of them said she stopped us. Then she asked, while looking back at you, "Where is that nigger going?"

They assured her that I was with them. At that point she began to apologize. Of course, that apology rolled over to me as I approached the facilities.

Out of all the humiliating things that have happened to me because of the color of my skin, this had to be the one that hurt the most. Here was someone of my color. Working at a blue-collar job, on the low-end. Who judged me to be lower than she herself was. In fact, she judged us both.

For the rest of the evening it was very difficult to communicate with my crew members. They tried to assure me that everything was fine. It was an embarrassing situation to have someone of my ethnic group degrading me.

This time I was hurt deeper than ever. In fact, I have never been hurt like that again.

Collection of Miscellaneous Stories

There are times when a story I have heard fits the situation better than a personal experience. These are some of those stories.

We May Never Meet Again

A smartly dressed middle-aged woman was returning from a shopping spree in the city of Philadelphia. She was returning home after shopping at the well-known large department stores. She carried several shopping bags which were bulging with Christmas gifts.

She was snuggled in her fur trimmed coat. Winter in Philly could be quite brutal. As she neared the train station, she noticed the clock. She was surprised to find that she had plenty of time before her train left for the suburbs.

It just so happened that there was a coffee shop right next to the train station. How convenient it would be to stop in and warm-up on a cup of hot coffee. She entered the small coffee shop and placed her bags in one of the booths. She proceeded to the counter and ordered a cup of coffee and on the way back she noticed there were delicious looking pies.

She grabbed a piece of pie and proceeded to her table where she placed her coffee and pie. Realizing that she needed silverware, she returned to the counter where she picked up a spoon and returned to her booth.

To her surprise there was now a black gentleman sitting at her table about to eat her pie. The man was approximately her age. He wore a large winter down jacket. On the edge of the table he had placed a knitted cap with a ball on top. She could see that he was a blue-collar worker. That is, if he did have a job.

She sat down opposite the man and pulled her pie toward her. The man looked at her and pulled the pie back to himself. She was not giving up. She pulled the pie back to herself. The man was not giving up either and he returned the favor by returning it to his side of the table.

This went on for three more times. Finally, the lady took her fork and cut a piece of pie and placed it in her mouth. She was shocked when the man mirrored her actions, pulling the pie back and putting a piece of pie in his mouth.

The lady was really starting to fume at this point. She pulled the pie back again, taking another bite. He repeated her action. This continued until the pie was finished.

They looked at each other. The man then went and pulled the cup of coffee in front of them. He picked up the sugar packets. Looking at her she replied by putting up two fingers. The man took two packs of sugar, opened them and emptied them into the coffee cup.

He lifted the creamer. She nodded, and he poured some cream into the coffee cup. Then they shared a cup of coffee.

As they finished the coffee, the lady realized that it was time for her to leave. She gathered her gloves, patted her lips with the napkin and left. Entering the train station, she looked for the track that the train would be leaving from.

Then it happened. She realized that she had left her bags at the coffee shop. She ran back to the coffee shop as quickly as she could, entered the coffee shop and looked at the table. The empty plate and coffee cup were still there.

The man was gone and so were her bags. She was very upset with herself and began to pace up and down the restaurant. As she did so she happened to notice another booth with her bags. As she'd left them.

Not only that, but on the table sat an untouched piece of pie and cup of coffee. This was the table on which she had placed her pie and coffee. She had just shared a piece of pie and coffee with a stranger.

Grabbing her bags, she rushed to the train station. Locating the track for train departure, she entered the train car just in time. Having a moment to relax, she realized that she had been willing to share a coffee with a man of much lesser means.

How many times have we judged people wrongly? Based on how they look and our beliefs we tend to profile them. At a later time, we find that not all of our assumptions were true.

The question is, are we willing to change our beliefs to confirm their truth? In the case of this lady she truly had believed this man was stealing her piece of pie. She stood her ground and in return she allowed him to stand his ground. In doing so they found common ground.

They will never be friends. But finding common ground allowed them to share a moment of spiritual delight. I try not to judge people based on how I feel in the moment. That does not say that my feelings are not real. But they could be tainted by the perfume or cologne being worn.

I may not like the color of their clothes or even the style. But they do not make up the character of the person. I do have to share that I have made many mistakes. I have wrongly judged someone who later turned out to be a very good friend.

You can communicate with or without words. Positive or negative statements.

From a past A&E broadcast, more than 25 years ago.

The Power of Small Deeds

One of the inspiring stories I use for a Toastmasters meeting begins with a woman from an African village. She had recently lost her only child. She decided to visit the village's great shaman to ask why the gods had taken her child. The shaman replied that life comes with pain. She became furious and demanded that he bring her child back.

After much thought the shaman agreed. He would bring the child back if she would bring him a mustard seed from a village home where pain had never been experienced.

Thinking this was going to be an easy requirement, she first went to the richest family in the village. Surely these people, being wealthy, would not have known any pain. She explained her quest. They replied that they would gladly give her a mustard seed.

They shared with her that it was difficult to find friends. Everybody wanted something from them. In fact, some of their best friends had stolen from them. Others, when they didn't give them money, ended the relationship. Their children did not know how to handle the wealth and were constantly getting into trouble, thinking they could pay their way out. Their son was killed in a fight over gambling debts.

Leaving empty-handed she proceeded to a middle-class family. They too had their problems. She then went to the poor section of the village. There she sat down with a woman who had little or nothing. She began to explain that she did not have any food for her child. Her second child was sick with fever, the roof leaked over their heads and her husband had run off.

The woman saw such destitution that she wanted to offer hope. She began to gather food and bring it back to the poor family. She asked her husband to repair the roof and she gave comfort and medicine to the sick child.

She was so involved in working and helping she forgot about her own problems. From then on, she went from house to house to see if she could provide any assistance. There was always someone worse off than she was.

Credit: *Daily Motivations for African-American Success*
Dennis Kimbro

Sun Talker

Article from local Toastmasters newsletter

Speaker Spotlight: Ron "Mel" Melvin, DTM
by Esther Lenssen, ACB, ALB, *SunTalker* Editor

Ronald E. Melvin, DTM, also known as "Mystic Mel", is an international humorous speaker who combines his presentations and workshops with entertaining magic. In his speeches he tells unique stories that encompass life coaching, inspiration and humor. Mel has been a Toastmaster since 1992 and his public speaking experience spans more than 30 years.

Results of hard work and dedication

Last year, Mel was one of the nine finalists of the Toastmasters World Championship of Public

Speaking, which was held in Orlando, FL, in August. In April 2013, Mel joined Area 44 Governor Gene Kowalski, ACG, ALB, and EduSpeakers' VP Education Lynn Kruse, ACB, ALB, at Goliath Radio 1380 AM to promote the Division D International Speech and Table Topics Contest on the "Via Report" with host Roland Via. Here are a few of the questions Roland asked and Mel's answers:

Roland Via: Did you think when you first joined Toastmasters that you'd be there [at the finals of the Toastmasters World Championship of Public Speaking]?
Mel: I always wanted to be there. To say that I'd get there... It is always a struggle.

Roland Via: Yeah, the desire is one thing, the ability to do it another.
Mel: I knew I could do it. It's just getting there... It's taken a lot of time, it's not an easy task to do. It takes a lot of time; a lot of effort and you have to get a lot of support from the other Toastmasters.

Roland Via: And that's one of the reasons that Toastmasters is so successful. It's not a "me" group, it's a "we" group more than anything else. Would that be correct?
Mel: I'd say that you're absolutely right with that. We in Toastmasters want everyone to succeed. That's the whole idea. Each club was started by people like the new people who walk in the door each week. They're

there to show that they did it, and now we can help you do that.

Roland Via: That makes all the sense in the world. So, you had to work long and hard on that, but Toastmasters gives you the tools, the ability and the training to move yourself along. As long as you have that master ingredient and that's the desire to want to do it.

Mel: Yes, and when you have the desire, along with that must come the desire to get support from others. You can't do this alone. Speaking is not only you; you can speak to a wall and be very good...

Roland Via [interrupts]: I know, I do that every day between 2 and 4 o' clock.

Mel [laughs]

Roland Via [laughs]: I talk to a lot of walls... Sometimes I laugh at myself...

Mel [laughs]: But you know, the other part is... who's receiving it. If you can get other people to understand and receive and feel the emotions that you're putting into your speech that makes it a good speech.

Roland Via: But what makes it a good speech is this "when you put the emotions and everything into it, people can tell when you're connecting with yourself, and that's a rare commodity sometimes. Whenever we look at politicians, for instance, and we're looking at their campaign speeches, sometimes their body language and the emphasis they put on words are probably more important than anything else. And here I am on radio moving my hands... But that does make a difference, right?

Mel: "It does make a difference, but I'm going to tell you a secret about speaking. It is when you can make the receiver feel what you want. You see, I can feel anything, but if I can't transfer that to you, your mind will start to wander. That's what I want to do. I want you to feel any emotion that I'm trying to share."

Roland Via: How do you get the listener to feel?

Mel: By telling them a story that they can relate to. You don't want to tell them a fully detailed story, because now they're trying to think of what you're feeling. Give them enough that they can feel from their own experience what it was like.

For example, remember the time that you were scared when you were going down the street and all of a sudden, a car veered off the street and onto the sidewalk. What was that like? That's what I'm trying to do. I don't want you to see exactly what I see, but what you see that makes you feel that way. I'm trying to steal your emotions, bring them up.

I was one of the listeners who called in to ask Mel questions live on the show. After I asked him for his advice about how to overcome any potential fears of taking part in a speaking contest and why he participated, Roland Via added the following question:

Roland Via: Do you encourage the failure points, where you say, "I cannot learn how to do it right until I'm doing it wrong and understand that I'm still alive, I'm still breathing, and people are still smiling and listening to me?"

Mel: No...

Roland Via [interrupts, surprised]: No?

Mel: ...there's no failure. Every failure is a learning element. You learn not to do it that way. It's not a failure. You just say, "Oops, that didn't work, let me try this one over here." I don't like to use [the word] "failure." That's a long story.

At Toastmasters I talk about how I was raised in a family as the failure. Therefore, Toastmasters has been a way for me to build up my own confidence, because I'm a shy person in my own way. I don't feel that I'm up to the standards of other people. But let's get back to this contest...

Roland Via [interrupts]: He's wrong by the way, everybody, he's dead wrong, but nonetheless [laughs], if you feel that way, Mel, okay, you can feel that way...

Mel [laughs]: When you're in your own club, your club loves you and they don't want to do anything to stop you from coming back again. But are you growing? [...] Where I learned the most was when I took my speech for the contest and went to other clubs and they beat me over the head. Sometimes I went home almost in tears. How could they hate that speech? How could they find that wrong? But I took it and I said, "Wait a minute. If they're feeling that way, that means if I go to a contest, somebody else is going to feel that way. How do I change it?" And I kept getting better at it that way. So, go to the contests. Compete. Take the things that you find that don't work, rewrite them. You'll make it.

Palm Coast Observer

By: Brian McMillan Executive Editor

PALM COAST - It was the kind of rain that would make any driver nervous, but it was particularly frightening for someone on a motorcycle: a wall of water, a Florida downpour limiting visibility to a couple of car lengths on Interstate 95. Ronald Melvin was a nervous wreck, surrounded by cars that could slam on their brakes or knock right into him as they changed lanes in the storm.

"It gets your heart pumping," Melvin recalled about that rainy ride in 2011. The rain pounded his glasses until finally, he decided to find safety under a bridge. He stopped, watching the geysers spray out from the passing cars. He wiped his face as the rain formed a curtain on either side of the bridge.

Shortly afterward, Bruce Wynne rode up to him on his motorcycle. Melvin had been following Wynne, and Wynne was frantic. He thought something terrible might have happened when he had looked back and couldn't see Melvin.

The two men were an unlikely riding partnership, Melvin recalled. Aside from both being in their 60s, they were opposites in almost every way, from their race to their tastes in food and music.

In fact, they didn't talk much. They just rode. But the friendship meant everything to Melvin. It helped pull him out of a dark phase of his life, when a heart condition had limited his physical mobility. He withdrew, felt helpless and suddenly confronted with his own mortality.

To make matters worse, a loss in federal funding resulted in him losing his job in Palm Coast.

Thanks to Wynne, though, he learned to rediscover a certain joy in life. They loved each other like brothers, and that look on Wynn's face said it all. The worried look at the thought that Melvin might have crashed in the rain.

A month later, however, a tragedy did occur: Melvin was leading Wynne on a ride along International Speedway Boulevard, and when he arrived at the next stoplight, he realized Wynne wasn't behind him anymore. He circled back in time to see the ambulance arrive, but nothing could be done.

Melvin's best friend had died in a crash with another motorcycle.

The loss sent Melvin in another emotional downward spiral. He stopped riding. He withdrew again. The last time it happened because of his heart troubles, and Wynne had helped him out of it. Without Wynne, where could he turn?

Common Ground: My road to the International Speech Contest

One way Mel discovered to cope was through Toastmasters, an organization that teaches public speaking skills. He wrote a speech about his friendship with Wynne, inspiring people to build on common ground.

"To love others, you have to love yourself," Melvin said. "That's the gauge you're working from, if you want to love others as yourself."

And he discovered that he was good at delivering this speech, which included a magic trick to capture the attention of his audience. He entered competitions and won. He ultimately won a national title and was qualified for the international competition in Florida against eight other toastmasters from around the world, out of an original pool of 30,000.

But there was one problem: The contestants had to write new speeches for the championship. Melvin had to let go of his familiar stories about Wynne and find another experience to tell.

The fear of dying.

The new speech ended up being about a flight instructor who once gave Melvin a flying lesson. The instructor held up a pencil and told Melvin he wanted to show him that he could make it float. The idea was to take the two-seat plane straight up into the sky and then quickly dive back toward the ground, suspending the pencil in the air momentarily. Melvin was so nervous as he was ascending that he gripped the seat at his sides. Inadvertently, he un-clipped Steve's seat belt.

Therefore, when the plane made its dramatic turn, not only the pencil floated but also the pilot, who smacked his head on the roof of the cockpit and was knocked out cold.

Melvin was there, feeling alone, sick to his stomach, high above the earth, slowly tilting downward.
"What did you do?" I asked Melvin, my eyes wide. I met him at the studios of WNZF after he appeared on "Free For All Friday" with David Ayers.

Melvin, a short and stout, unassuming man, laughed. As it turned out, the moment of terror was just that, a moment. The pilot recovered consciousness and safely landed the plane. No miraculous landing required for Melvin.

When they got out of the plane, Melvin recalled, the two men started laughing. "We never laughed so hard at the fear of dying," he said. "He taught me to laugh at problems, to find the side that is funny."

Melvin dramatically told the story in the studio last week, but unfortunately, the day of the competition in August 2012, his heart wasn't in it. He felt he didn't perform like he should have, and he lost. This sent him into yet another downward spiral. The success of reaching the international championships in Orlando faded, and all he could think about was losing.

"I hadn't done a good enough job," he recalled. "My friends from Toastmasters were cheering me on. It was in Florida! Home crowd. This year, it's in Dubai. And I blew it. I blew it."

"Get up and do something"

Afterward, people asked him to give his speech again about Wynne, and he couldn't do it. In fact, he stopped going to Toastmasters altogether.

"I didn't want to talk about Bruce," he said. "I didn't want to talk about whether I was competing again next year."

He felt the loss of his friend weigh on him, and he realized he still hadn't fully come to terms with Wynne's death. The speech had been a crutch, and losing the competition was like having someone kick away that crutch.

As a former firefighter in Pennsylvania, Melvin was a member of a group called Knights of the Inferno Motorcycle Club. Here was a new set of friends who all knew what Wynn's death meant to Melvin.

They said, "Do you think Bruce would want you to feel this way?" Melvin recalled. "I realized I had to take care of me."

So, he rode his motorcycle around the block near his Palm Coast home, trying to overcome the fear that someone was going to blindside him from a side street.

But soon, he began venturing out of his neighborhood again, and in the past six months, Melvin has begun to reconstruct.

Now, at 67, he is ready to begin again. He is riding in the second-annual poker run to benefit the Frank Celico Foundation, which is planned for April 19.

He decided he wants to become an inspirational speaker. His message: developing inner strength to build personal power.

On a chance meeting, Ayres invited him to be a guest on "Free For All Friday." He wasn't sure what to expect, but he was determined to take advantage of any chance to get exposure for his new venture.

"People don't know what to do, so they sit there," Melvin said. "But even if you do the wrong thing, you at least know you're doing something."

He's exploring social media, setting up webinars, attending a branding seminar, seeking partnerships with magicians, under the stage name "Mystic Mel." He's seeking opportunities to speak at clubs and groups to see where this will take him. "I just decided to get up and go," he said, "and look at what happened. Look at me and you," he said, pointing to me, as we wrapped up our interview at the studio. "Look what happened. Get up and do something."

That's what Bruce Wynne would tell him to do. And as he rides through town now, Melvin has a smile on his face. It's like his friend is right behind him again.

http://www.palmcoastobserver.com/article/ride-lifetime

Reporter: Brian McMillan

How to Win the Toastmasters World Championship of Public Speaking by Jeremey Donovan, International Speech Critique

What follows is Jeremy Donovan's evaluation and analysis of my international competition speech. I used several personal stories in constructing my speech, some of which are in this book. I highly recommend Donovan's book for competitive speakers. I am grateful to Jeremy for the right to use contents from his *How to Win the Toastmasters World Championship of Public Speaking*.

Jeremy Donovan's Evaluation

After two Anglo-Saxons, Ronald [Melvin] was the first person of color to take the stage. Over the course of the day, the audience would discover that two-thirds of the finalists were non-White. But, this fact likely went completely unnoticed because Toastmasters International has what is likely the most diverse membership of any top-tier service organization.

Toastmasters is gender-blind--52 percent of members are female, and 48 percent are male. Toastmasters is age-blind--the average member age is 45.8 years, but 25 percent of members are eighteen to twenty-four. Toastmasters is income-blind, education-blind, and disability-blind. The same goes for race, religion, and sexual orientation.

Centered on his relationship with his white, Jewish best friend Steve Eisenberg, Ronald's speech was a snapshot of the Toastmasters' diversity experience in miniature. Learning from Steve's reactions to increasingly challenging circumstances, Ronald has a revelation tied to the core virtue of positivity. He learns to respond to disaster with laughter. Reliving a personal epiphany is among the very best ways to tell an inspirational story.

Ronald E. Melvin opened with an audience-participation exercise that is known to magicians as David Copperfield's arm-twist illusion. [The] surprised audience members, with their hands unable to rotate, let out their first big laugh just twenty-two seconds into the speech. Ronald would pile on another twenty-one laughs over the course of his six and a half minutes on stage, more than any other speaker in the contest. This is all the more impressive given that Ronald's story grew increasingly dark as he progressed. If you are going to give a speech about turning disaster into laughter, then you had better be funny.

With the laugh under his belt, Ronald revealed his core message by linking his magic trick with the audience's broader life experiences. "Sometimes you start out doing something innocent and you end up all twisted. All of those events don't have to be that way. Sometimes we can change disaster into laughter." If there is one nit to pick, it is that getting one's arms twisted is a tenuous metaphor for real-life disasters.

By doing a magic trick, one might logically have expected that Ronald would have used additional illusions to metaphorically demonstrate the lessons in his talk. Instead, he shifted into storytelling mode, which made his introduction feel a bit disconnected from the remainder of his speech.

Ronald completed the last sentence of his introduction--"Sometimes we can change disaster into laughter" --and then signaled his transition into the body of his speech in multiple ways.

First, he took a two-second pause. Second, he moved several steps to his left as he began to share a personal story about living in Rochester, Minnesota, in the 1980s. Ronald's movement appeared frenetic and unstructured. In fact, moving left just a few steps rather than a significant distance was evidence of this.

During his speech, Ronald covered three vignettes that occurred at different times and different physical locations. Hence, he had two options. He could have mapped the stage chronologically. This is the most common approach in Toastmasters and beyond. Since Western audiences read left to right, he should have started his story by moving to the audience's left rather than to his left. His second option would have been to lay out the stage like a map. This would have been more challenging, though not impossible, given that his locations were Minnesota, an airplane, and Florida.

In addition to pausing and moving, there are additional ways to clearly signal your speech transition. Ronald demonstrated one of them well and the other not as well. The one he did nicely was using language that indicates a turning point. He began the first part of the body of his speech with, "It was the 1980's; I was living in Rochester, Minnesota." Any major shift in plot, setting, time, or character signals a transition. In addition, there is a wide range of words and phrases that have just as strong an impact.

Ronald's only missed opportunity to signal a transition was that he did not noticeably shift his vocal delivery. Throughout the speech, he maintained a passionate conversational style that was generally loud, fast, and accentuated by pauses. Transitions are most effective when they have a large contrast. Hence, Ronald could have shifted his voice to slower and softer during the transition. In spite of that, with all the other best practices he applied, the audience had no doubt that he had moved from the introduction into the body of his speech.

All great speeches have an introduction, body and conclusion. Beyond that constraint, there are endless opportunities to creatively build the narrative structure for a speech.

In broad brush strokes, Ronald Melvin constructed his speech in the following way. In his introduction, Ronald delivered a problem statement--sometimes life throws us challenges and we need to choose how to respond. The body of his speech consisted of three distinct stories. The first story is set in the 1980s, when the speaker attends his friend Steve's wedding.

The point of this story is that we can turn embarrassment into laughter. The second story, set slightly later in time, relates Ronald's experience of riding in Steve's airplane. The point of this story is that we can turn accidents into laughter. The third story recounts Ronald's experience at the end of Steve's life. The point of this story is that we can turn tragedy into laughter. Finally, he concluded by driving home his core message: "Les Brown says, 'If you get knocked down, get knocked down on your back so you can see which way to get up.' I say to you, when you get up, get up laughing and turn disaster into laughter."

Beyond the risk he took in opening with a magic trick--which could equally have helped him or hurt him--Ronald's speech was extremely well constructed. He made a clear choice to tell three separate stories that were cobbled together by virtue of many best practices. The stories were chronologically linear in time. Each of the stories had the same characters. And, most elegantly, the stories reinforced the theme of turning disaster into laughter in increasingly high-stakes situations.

Let's deconstruct Ronald's first story to illustrate why it is indeed a story and not simply a first act. In Ronald's ordinary world, he is the lone person of color living in Rochester, Minnesota during the 1980s. The good news is that he has made a great friend, Steve, whom he first met at a business meeting. Act 1 ends and Act 2 begins innocuously enough when Ronald is invited to Steve's wedding. Hilarity ensues when the bride and groom are announced as Mr. and Mrs. Jackson. The problem is that Steve's last name is Eisenberg! The tension reaches its climax at the end of Act 2 when Ronald reclaims his gift from the Jackson party's table. Act 3 establishes a new normal of close friendship and laughter between Ronald and Steve. With all conflict resolved and the moral of turning disaster into laughter fully revealed, the first story is complete. By telling his stories in standard chronological order, Ronald delivered a textbook example of a linear progression.

Ronald, along with the overwhelming majority of past Toastmasters champions, told his stories from the first-person perspective. Over the course of Ronald's stories, the audience got a picture of his strengths, his desires, and his flaws--the three elements of character development. As for strengths, we know that he is both compassionate and sociable. By mentioning with a humorous tone that he was the lone person of color in a city of 110,000, he reveals his desire to fit in. His flaw links to the core message: Ronald, like most people, get anxious in the face of disaster.

Just as the speaker [Ronald Melvin] gained a valuable gift from someone else, the speaker pays that gift forward to the audience.

Ronald Melvin clearly had this principle in mind when he chose his friend, Steve Eisenberg, as his mentor. Steve showed Ronald how to laugh in the face of disaster, even in Steve's darkest hour. Just as Luke Skywalker had Obi-Wan Kenobi in Star Wars, Ronald had Steve. And just as Luke had to lose his mentor, Ronald had to lose Steve to stand on his own and be able to laugh in the face of future disaster.

Ronald's speech as a mixture of dialogue with subtext and dialogue that is "on the nose." The very first line of dialogue is of the latter variety: "My name's Steve. I know how you feel. I go and recruit at minority colleges, and even though I'm treated well, I still feel uncomfortable." Steve's transparent emotional disclosure did feel somewhat realistic and served to efficiently highlight a common bond with the speaker. Ronald's response to Steve--"Welcome to my world!"--was richly laden with the subtext of what it is like to be a minority.

Dialogue with subtext is also one of the key ways to get laughs from an audience. The wittiest line of dialogue in Ronald's speech comes when Steve is about to take him up in an airplane and asks: "Mel, have you ever seen a pencil float?" This line is immediate foreshadowing. Ronald follows the dialogue with action, another best practice in storytelling, when he adds: "With that, he grabbed the controls and pulled it back. The plane went into climb, it started coughing and spluttering."

Would you take your hand and put it out front of you like this, palm inside? Yes, everybody, stick it out there. Very good. Would you now point your thumb down to the ground? Very good. Taking the left hand and placing it over, locking the fingers. Yup, you've got it right, you've got it right. Okay, one, two, three, turn them over. Very good. Contest Chair, Toastmasters and guests. That's life.

Sometimes you start out doing something innocent and you end up all twisted. All of those events don't have to be that way. Sometimes we can change disaster into laughter.

It was the 1980s. I was living in Rochester, Minnesota. 110,000 people and three of color. Me, myself and I. I went to a business meeting and a gentleman came up to me and said, "my name is Steve." I know how you feel. I go and recruit at minority colleges, and even though I'm treated well, I still feel uncomfortable.

I said, "Welcome to my world!" We bonded that time and became very good friends. He invited me to his wedding. Beautiful wedding. I went to the reception just in time to see two young ladies walking in the door. Wine, women and song. They went down the hallway and they had a number of these receptions going on. They went to a table and there were their names, and I saw mine. I picked it up and followed them in. I went up and I placed my gift there and went to the assigned table but I was surprised.

All the chairs were taken, but they were so gracious. They parted, and the waiter went to get me a chair and I went to the open bar. Well then, the announcer started to introduce the bridal party. After all the bridal party was introduced, the announcer said "for the first time, I'd like to introduce Mr. and Mrs. Jackson"

"Jackson? Who's Jackson? Steve's name is Eisenberg!" I ran outside and I took a look and in that moment of clarity I saw that the signs were facing opposite ways and I had went in the wrong door.

Okay, I'll go in the right door. Oh, my gift! Just as I turned around, I looked at the announcer coming out and I explained my situation. He said, "Well, go in and get your gift."

I said, "What's wrong with you Mr. Willis?"

Well, at this point I said I'm not going in there by myself. He took me in, and I got my gift and I followed him closely back out. When Steve saw me, he grabbed me and hugged me, said, "Mel, it's so good to see you!" I told him what happened, he began to laugh. Then I told him about the gift. He laughed harder. He had turned disaster into laughter.

Later on, he took me up in a plane and it was like being in a Volkswagen with wings. As we were up there, I guess he was getting bored because he reached into his pocket, pulled out a pencil and placed it on the dash. He said, "Mel, have you ever seen a pencil float?" With that, he grabbed the controls and pulled it back. The plane went into a climb, it started coughing and spluttering. At that point, he shoved the controls and the plane went in a dive. I went from grabbing this to pushing that.

I looked over at Steve and he was knocked out, but it was floating. Folks, that's when I heard a little girl screaming. Yes, it was me. They say your life flashes in front of you. Not mine, it stood perfectly still, except for that little light that said "boy, you're going to die."

At that point the plane started to level off. I looked back at Steve, he was rubbing his head. When he finally got the controls, he said, "You know this plane is trained to fly normally when nobody touches the controls."

"Yea, thanks for letting me know."

Now he brings the plane down to land. Bringing it in to a stop, he reaches down and notices that his seat belt had been unhooked. I had done it when I threw my hands up and he had hit his head on the top of the plane. We started to laugh. We laughed. I made the mistake of telling him about the little girl screaming. But anyway, we had turned disaster into laughter.

I moved to Florida. I tried to get him to come see me and finally one day he said, "Mel, I can't, I have Lou Gehrig's disease." This disease robs you of your muscles and your nerves.

A couple of weeks later, I got a call from his wife saying, "If you want to see him, you better come now." I took the first plane to Minnesota, and I walked in the house and there was Steve in this contraption that his wife had to use to lift and move him around the house.

I sat there on the sofa and I started to cry. "Oh, my friend, Steve. Why you?"

Steve said, "Mel, do you remember when you went to the wrong reception?"

He was changing disaster into laughter. We started to laugh about all the bloopers I had done while I was in

Rochester, until he couldn't breathe again, and his wife ran over to grab him.

I grabbed him, and I hugged him as hard as I could because he could not hold me.

We can't cure everything with laughter, but we can feel better. Why do we wait until people are gone before we talk about their bloopers? We start off saying something nice, "Oh, that Mel looked good up on stage until he fell off."

Les Brown says, "If you get knocked down, get knocked down on your back so you can see which way to get up. I say to you, when you get up, get up laughing and turn disaster into laughter.
[End of speech]

With "turn disaster into laughter," Ronald Melvin crafted a catchphrase that is about as textbook-perfect as they come. Like Andrew Kneebone's [speaker number one] it is short and rhythmic like Stuart Pink [speaker number two] Ronald used it as his title and reinforced the message in each part of his speech. But, he did something that his two predecessors did not. He made it action-centric to the point where everybody in the room could take it with them and apply it when they left.

Ronald E. Melvin had an extremely well-constructed three-part narrative structure he used to deliver a compelling message that we must turn disaster into laughter. He was also the funniest speaker of the day, with an eye-popping 3.3 laughs per minute. However, the magic trick he did in his introduction was rather disconnected from the rest of his speech. Many audience members and judges were likely left stunned, momentarily trying to figure out how he did the trick.

Central message(s) Positivity

Duration 6.58 Minutes

Words per minute 153
Laughs per minute 3.3

About the Author

Ronald Melvin, AKA "Mystic Mel", retired from IBM after 30 years of service. He spent the next seven years as Resource Director for two United Ways, one in Rochester, Minnesota the other in Volusia-Flagler County, Florida. In 2009, he began a new career at the Center for Management and Employee Leadership (CMEL) in Palm Coast, Florida, training Federal Aviation Administration (FAA) personnel in management skills.

Mystic Mel

He served as the Chair of the Human Rights Commission for both the City of Rochester and

Olmsted County, Minnesota, for more than three years. He was the first to receive the "You Made a Difference" award from Olmsted County and received the Small Business of the Year award from the Rochester Area Chamber of Commerce.

Mystic Mel began his speaking career in 1984 while being employed by IBM. By providing informative, educational and entertaining presentations and workshops, he was sought by many companies and organizations to speak about diversity and was inspired by these opportunities to start his own speaking and training company. Throughout his speaking career he has made presentations to a variety of audiences, including IBM, Mayo Clinic, American Job Corp, NASCAR and the Unitarian Universalist Society, to name just a few.

During his years in Minnesota, Mystic Mel studied the art of magic and includes his passion for magic and speaking in his presentations for both profit and non-profit organizations.

He became a Distinguished Toastmaster, the highest level in that organization, in October of 2008. In August 2012, he was a regional champion and one of nine finalist in the Toastmasters International Speech Contest, competing against over 33,000 contestants from around the world.

Positions and affiliations have included membership in Lions Club, both in Rochester, Minnesota, where he served as President, and Ormond Beach, Florida. Treasurer for the Conklin Center for the Blind, five years as a volunteer fireman in Conshohocken, Pennsylvania, a certified sailing instructor and a member of the Leads into the Future entrepreneur group of Palm Coast, Florida, demonstrates his wide-range of interests and involvement in the communities in which he has lived and worked.

He also has been featured in numerous publications and in media – an article, *How to Win the Toastmaster World Championship*, *Flagler County Observer*, in the *Daytona Beach News Journal*, an article in *Real Talker*, *Rochester Post Bulletin* and ABC-FOX news.

He holds a Master's Degree in Management from St. Mary's University, Winona, Wisconsin.

For presentations and workshops, Mystic Mel can be contacted at Mysticalmel@gmail.com.

www.ingramcontent.com/pod-product-compliance
Lightning Source LLC
Chambersburg PA
CBHW071609080526
44588CB00010B/1069